D1094337

Learning to Learn

Ways to Nurture Your Child's Intelligence

Learning to Learn

Ways to Nurture Your Child's Intelligence

Angela Browne-Miller

Foreword by
Phyllis R. Magrab, Ph.D.
and
Martha M. Kendrick, Esq.

 **INSIGHT BOOKS**

Plenum Press • New York and London

Library of Congress Cataloging in Publication Data

Browne-Miller, Angela, 1952–

    Learning to learn: ways to nurture your child's intelligence / Angela Browne-
Miller: foreword by Phyllis R. Magrab and Martha M. Kendrick
        p.   cm.
    Includes bibliographical references and index.
    ISBN 0-306-44647-2
    1. Learning. 2. Cognition in children. I. Magrab, Phyllis R. II. Kendrick,
Martha M. III. Title.
LB1060.B77 1994   93-50219
370.15'23—dc20   CIP

ISBN 0-306-44647-2

© 1994 Plenum Press, New York
A Division of Plenum Publishing Corporation
233 Spring Street, New York, N.Y. 10013-1578

An Insight Book

Printed in the United States of America

To my daughter,
Evacheska Veda Lahaila deAngelis Browne-Miller

Sed quando submoventa erit ignorantia…
(When the time comes for the removal of ignorance…)

      —MICHEL DE NOSTREDAME (NOSTRADAMUS), 1555

Multa debetur puero reverentia.
(We must revere the young.)

      —MARIA MONTESSORI, 1952

Foreword

Raising a child is one of the most challenging processes anyone can undertake. Whether it is as a parent or as a teacher, involvement in a young person's development is no small responsibility. We know, almost instinctively, that what we do and do not do with a child today can affect what that child does and does not accomplish tomorrow and later in life.

And there is no single "right way" to be involved, no one standard approach to parenting and teaching, that is guaranteed to produce happy and high-functioning citizens from the children we raise. This is as it should be. We would not want all of our child-rearing practices dictated to us in great detail by some overseeing organization. Even teachers, who face more regulation than parents, are left a respectable amount of latitude when it comes to teaching style. When it comes to raising children, we cherish whatever freedom we have to make our own decisions according to our own values, tastes, and preferences.

In our very complex, diverse, and demanding world, families and schools do the best they can to prepare young people for adulthood. However, too many of our children grow up without tapping their true mental potentials. Why is this so?

What this book, *Learning to Learn*, explains is that some rethinking of—or new thinking about—intelligence is necessary. Whatever brain capacity a child is born with, it can be greatly enhanced when purposefully cultivated. This cultivation must be aimed at encouraging what the author, Angela Browne-Miller, describes as the expression of mental ability. With concerted effort on the many levels that Dr. Browne-Miller addresses in this book (including the home–school transition, the family environment, the physical environment, the spiritual environment, and the attitudes regarding problem solving and struggles), markedly positive differences in a child's expression of his or her mental ability can result.

Learning to Learn demonstrates that we can teach our children's minds to work well—to learn to learn. Our children can come to see their brains and their minds as tools that, when used well, can perform well. Dr. Browne-Miller introduces the concept of consciousness technology here as something that parents can develop in themselves and then teach to their children. Children can become highly conscious of their consciousnesses. They can bring the workings of their minds to their own attentions and then direct these workings in a way that we are just beginning to appreciate.

Now, more than ever, we are confronted with an increasingly apparent disparity in educational, occupational, and career opportunity. What this means is that, for a variety of reasons, some people learn more in school, test higher on exams, find themselves in higher-paying jobs, and develop more satisfactory careers for themselves than do others. If there is a way to extend these opportunities to a broader range of the population, it is essential to begin preparing them for these opportunities when they are children. We are at that time in history when the dissemination of the consciousness technology described in this book can have a very positive social and political impact.

This book is easily read, easily understood, and a valuable resource to both professionals and families. Dr. Browne-Miller, through this book, presents a message of great hope and self-help for parents and educators today, and for future generations.

PHYLLIS R. MAGRAB, PH.D.   MARTHA M. KENDRICK, ESQ.

Professor of Pediatrics   *Patton, Boggs & Blow*
Georgetown University Medical Center   *Washington, D.C.*
Washington, D.C.

Preface

Astounding universes, vast and intricate, chaotic and orderly, foreign and familiar, are available to each and every one of us. All we have to know is how to use our minds. All we have to do is think and think well.

But who will parent our mental potentials into full realization? Who will guide us on the journeys of thought required to travel to such new places? In the end, we are our own captains, our own teachers. No one else can push us to those towering pinnacles of expression and achievement, to the heights of thought of which each of us is capable.

We are so alone in a world hungry for real mentoring, true intellectual guidance, sensitive personal tutoring in the science of the mind. But our children are not. They have us—their parents and teachers—their elders. They have us for but a few years before they become us.

The mind of a young person is so very precious and special. In that mind are housed the universes to which future generations can travel. In that mind are awesome paths of thought—mental workings so exotic that only the future will find a place for them.

The wealth of mental ability locked away in a child's mind is immeasurable. All we can do to estimate it is to help the child find the key that will unlock his or her own mental vault.

Despite our great interests in education, we tend to overlook the more subtle aspects of children's cognitive development. It is our attitudes regarding the realization of our children's mental abilities that can make or break their intelligences. The care and feeding of a child's mind is some of the most important work we will ever do. It is some of the greatest love we will ever give. It is, perhaps, the guarantee of our immortality. We live on through the minds of the next generation.

ANGELA BROWNE-MILLER

Tiburon, California

Acknowledgments

I wish to acknowledge the many children, parents, and teachers who have instructed me in the precious workings of their minds during my research for this book. I also wish to acknowledge the great teachers that I have had the privilege of being instructed by, including Gregory Bateson, Bernard Gifford, West Churchman, Ken Norris, Leo Zeff, and, most of all, my father, Lee Winston Browne, who could not be on this planet for the publication of this book. Lee explored some of the highest realms of mental functioning possible for human beings.

And I cannot forget to thank my three closest family members, who have lived with me as I have written almost ten books: my brave husband, Richard Louis Miller, who has been willing to be married to an author who tends to become lost in her work and mesmerized by her computers (to put it mildly); my adventurous stepdaughter, Sarana Miller, who has moved away to college and now reports back to me from the front line of higher education; and my astounding young daughter, Evacheska Browne-Miller, who has taught me more than anyone about how a child learns to think and about what really goes on in a young and pure mind. Evacheska's illustrations are included at the beginning of each chapter in this book and are signed "EBM."

Contents

Introduction to Cognitive Potential

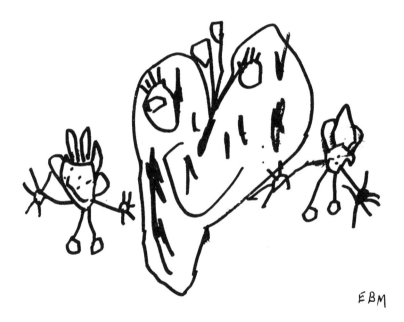

EBM

Knowledge is power.

—Old adage

> They waited patiently for what seemed a very long time, stamping in the snow to keep their feet warm. At last they heard the sound of slow shuffling footsteps approaching the door from the inside. It seemed, as the Mole remarked to the Rat, like someone walking in carpet slippers that were too large for him and down at heel; which was intelligent of Mole, because that was exactly what it was.

—Kenneth Grahame,
The Wind in the Willows

What is intelligence? Is it a gift or something that one works very hard to develop? If intelligence is a gift, how does one get it? Is one born with it or does some wonderful school teacher come along and plant it in one's mind? Are we stuck with the level of intelligence with which we are born? If not, if one's intelligence level is determined after birth, then: Can we raise intelligence during childhood? Can parents raise their children's intelligence?

These are good questions. Yet the intelligence we seek to raise is elusive. Researchers offer a variety of definitions of intelligence, many of them conflicting. The definitions range from genetic and biological to environmental to the combinations of these definitions on which most researchers agree to varying degrees. [1] They include a single form of intelligence, such as that defined by the standard I.Q., or "intelligence quotient," tests, and, in contrast to the single I.Q., multiple forms of intelligence, or "multiple intelligences," such as those suggested by Professor Howard Gardner at Harvard University. [2]

CONTROVERSY OVER INTELLIGENCE

There has been a great deal of social and political controversy over the theory that intelligence is biologically determined. [3] Jobs have been lost, reputations have been slandered, and major research funding has been canceled as a result of conflicting views regarding the genetic basis of intelligence. What the argument boils down to is this: We either can or cannot raise the level of someone's intelligence. If we cannot, no amount of social spending will lead to the correction of the unfair allocation of special (educational, economic, and social) opportunities available to the seemingly more intelligent persons. If we can, then we best commit to the social spending—in the form of educational and social programs—to do so.

If intelligence were entirely determined by biology, if it were entirely genetic, inherited, and fixed at birth, you would have no opportunity to change your intelligence level or that of your child. It would be set in stone or, more correctly, in genes. Some theorists, such as Arthur Jensen of the University of California at Berkeley, claim that there is a core intelligence, a single I.Q., an intelligence factor or intelligence "quotient" that is primarily inherited. Others, such as Leon Kamin at Princeton University, claim that society's labeling of some persons as more intelligent is a sociopolitical artifact and not at all a biologically determined fact. In Professor Kamin's view, academic and other mental achievement is not genetically predetermined at birth. This view says that the family and the sociopolitical environment determine intelligence and achievement in the world. The "better" the environment in which a child is reared, the "better" the child's mind will function, and the "better" the child will perform. (Much of this book is concerned with what can be made "better.")

Some biological theories of intelligence focus not so much on genetic inheritance but more on the notion of mental hardware: the neural connections in the brain. These fascinating theories are generating research that measures signal transmission—speed, intensity, and duration of electrical pulses—across the brain. Certain studies are concluding that the speed of this signal transmission across the brain is related to I.Q. level. [4] Whether the efficiency of the brain's signal transmission is biologically inherited or developed as a result of environmental stimulation is also subject to debate. As discussed in Chapters 8 and 14, some child development specialists argue that the efficiency of signal transmission across the brain is most influenced by the environment during *early* childhood, when the brain is developing its neural connections most rapidly, and that the quality and quantity of these connections can be best influenced in this early stage of life. If this is the case, then parents who start early can have a great deal of influence over their children's intelligence, including the speed at which their children think, their memory capacities, their specific abilities, and their concentration levels.

What about the basic issue of brain speed? Is thinking faster actually thinking better? Speedy signal transmission across the brain may make it possible for more connections to be made between old information already stored in the brain and fresh, incoming information. The more connections that are made, the more useful new information is, and the greater the likelihood that it will be used and remembered. Speedy transmission may therefore also improve information storage, that is, memory capability.

Memory is another area that seems to be related to intelligence. However, a person with a photographic memory may or may not be intelligent. Remembering every word on a page but being unable to think about these words is merely storing information well and not using it. Conversely, a poor memory is a hinderance to the development of mental ability. The more of what one learns one remembers, the more information and experience there is for one's brain to use.

Some researchers, such as Lloyd Humphreys, who served as a professor at several major universities and on the Board of

Directors of the American Psychological Association, have gone so far as to suggest that intelligence is merely an imaginary concept—that it does not exist. [5] Others, such as Howard Gardner, tell us that intelligence is an old-fashioned and politically loaded concept and that we should speak instead of various mental abilities. They contend that whether or not the word "intelligence" is used is less important than the idea that there are, indeed, varying degrees of mental competence in different areas. For example, according to theories of multiple intelligences, a high level of mathematical ability and a high level of verbal ability are not always found together and thus should not be measured together to form one I.Q. score. Verbal, mathematical, musical, artistic, spatial, leadership, planning, and other mental abilities are, according to some definitions of intelligence, specific and very separate intelligences. [6]

Whatever the specific area of intelligence or mental ability, it can be enhanced by concentration. As discussed in Chapter 9, concentration is critical in the development of mental ability. Parents of school children seem to know this when they ask, sometimes quite despairingly, whether or not their children can be taught to concentrate. The ability to concentrate is powerfully influenced by environment, in that distractions and practice-resisting distractions are provided by the environment. And because concentration affects mental ability, the environment that influences the development of that concentration also influences mental ability.

Let us focus on concentration for a moment. Most people, children as well as adults, have down times, or times when they are less able to focus on particular mental tasks. Sometimes, but quite rarely, birth defects, other organic brain disorders, and brain injuries disrupt and inhibit concentration. However, the inability to concentrate is usually related to a variety of simpler and more remediable conditions, including lack of interest in the subject, fatigue, distractions such as noise, and emotional problems. And often, children (and their parents) just do not know *how* to concentrate. Most of us have not had the benefit of any form of direct concentration training. If concentration empowers intelligence and if concentration can be taught, we have here at least one way to enhance our children's intelligence.

WHAT THIS BOOK IS ABOUT

In this book, I offer parents and teachers an attitude that promotes and inspires mental development in children of all ages. I discuss ways to think about intelligence and describe methods of raising children's mental abilities and intellectual performances. I provide examples of conversations, comments, and activities from which readers can generalize to their own lives and to the age-specific needs of their own children or students. The words "children" and "child" are often used loosely in this book, without restricting the focus to any particular age group, in hopes that these perspectives on intellectual development will be applied to young people from birth through at least the age of 18.

While I realize that most parents and teachers are already overburdened by the demands of modern life, I nevertheless contend that there must be a shifting of priorities. Yes, some of the activities I propose herein demand time. But others can be built into daily life, can be merged with existing activities. Ultimately, I am proposing a shift in the way we view our children—their use of time, their schedules, their play, their schoolwork, their interactions with us, and most of all, their spirits and their minds. I contend that children can be *inspired* to be intelligent. They can be taught how to concentrate. They can also be taught how to think, how to organize their thoughts, how to learn, and ultimately, they can be taught how to be intelligent. I describe an atmosphere that fosters the expression of intelligence, and I encourage attitudes that place value on intelligent and creative thinking and on the challenges and struggles that can bring about such thinking. The essence of my message is that adults—parents and teachers—can create an environment in which children's minds flourish. In this sense, I view mental ability and intelligence as being highly moldable and the expression of mental ability and intelligence as being profoundly influenced by environment. The fostering of a competent mind in a young person can become a challenging and rewarding way of life.

To create this reality, we must all develop our understanding of mental ability. In the next chapter, I discuss some of the folklore on mental ability and intelligence and the way in which common assumptions regarding intelligence affect our views of our own and our children's mental abilities. I then proceed, in Chapter 3, to delve deeper into the scientific views regarding intelligence and examine their influence on the education of mental ability.

Next, I focus on schools. In Chapter 4, I discuss modern education and intelligence, focusing on issues such as educational labeling and tracking and the identification of gifted children. In Chapter 5, I talk about what to look for when selecting preschools and schools for children with some special notes on abuse and neglect in these settings. In Chapter 6, I look at the transition the child makes from home to the educational setting, where "school success" and "school problems" emerge.

From the school setting, I move to the family environment, in Chapter 7, where I examine key characteristics of what I call "the nest." Here, I include my thinking about children and television. The physical aspects of the nest, or any place where a child spends time, are so critical that they are discussed separately in Chapter 8.

Then, I move on to more technical aspects of mental ability. First, I examine practical approaches to developing mental ability in young minds, in Chapter 9, where we look at strategy selection, concentration, memory, brain speed, and other functional elements of mental ability. In Chapter 10, I discuss the precious *ability* to learn and how children can actually *learn* to learn. In Chapter 11, which builds on Chapters 9 and 10, I suggest that we can teach children to think about thinking; we can develop their "control" knowledge.

It is only when the refining of mental ability is merged with the focusing of the spirit that the highest of mental potentials can be reached. Such a fantastic merging of forces can be inspired by making the mind highly conscious of the workings of its own suprastructure and of the creative responses of that suprastructure to the mental challenges and struggles of life. This is a heightened awareness—a new technology—that parents and teachers can offer young people. I therefore turn, in Chapter 12, to the development of conscious creativity in children through emphasis on specific processes such as association and inquiry, as well as by employing a new form of what we can call *consciousness technology*.

All efforts to train a young person's mind and spirit must take place in an atmosphere of high regard for the often fragile, but sometimes unflappable, self-esteem of a child. In Chapter 13, I explain that the importance of struggle is tied to the development of mental potential. In Chapter 14, I conclude with the notion that, in educating children, we are building not only the adults of tomorrow but also the future of the world. Indeed, a mind is a terrible thing to waste. And so is the future.

As a parent, you have a responsibility to your child. By this, I mean that you are responsible for a great deal of that child's development. Mental development begins at home, at birth, and probably even in the womb. Don't overlook the opportunity to actualize your child's potential. Your own child's mind is your most precious contribution to civilization.

As a teacher, you have a challenging responsibility to your students: You direct their learning processes in a way that builds specific abilities and develops a sense of the powers (or weaknesses) of these abilities. You also have the opportunity to help parents understand their roles in the realization of their children's mental potentials.

Whatever role we play in children's lives, our views regarding their education and their mental abilities will either cultivate or squelch a great and irreplaceable national resource: the mind of the next generation. It is our responsibility as parents, educators, and taxpayers to empower our children, to develop their intelligences, and to prepare them for a future we can only imagine.

Chapter 2

The Folklore on Intelligence

I grew up in poverty in a Black neighborhood in the South. For me and my brothers and sisters, intelligence was being smart enough to get out of there any way you could.
> —38-year-old chiropractic student

I remember being intelligent before I was a (glue) sniffer. I could solve math problems. Now I can't. I killed too many brain cells. I can't think in some ways at all anymore. I feel a part of my brain missing.
> —18-year-old ex-glue sniffer
> Learning-disabled program student

Being smart is doing what the teacher wants you to do. All the time.
> —8-year-old fourth grader

I'm smart because my mommy says so.
> —4-year-old preschool student

So you want to do everything you can to maximize your child's intelligence. But what is intelligence? Exactly what is it that you want to maximize? There are so many forms and definitions of intelligence that parents must decide for themselves what they think intelligence might be. Parents must also decide which aspects of intelligence they believe can actually be learned by their children.

UNDERSTANDING INTELLIGENCE IS IMPORTANT

Look around. Listen. What do people believe is intelligence? How do they recognize it? How do people classify the various types of intelligence? Our definitions of intelligence have a powerful effect on the types of mental ability we encourage in ourselves and our children.

Let us say, for the sake of discussion, that intelligence is some form of intellectual competence. All intellectual competence can be divided into two basic categories. One is material knowledge, or "expertise": book learning. The other category is control skill or "control knowledge": the *use* of book learning once it is learned. [1]

Our understanding of knowledge and intelligence has undergone marked transition in recent years. The notion of book learning, of the acquiring of information from books, has been around for so long that the phrase "he's got book learning" has become a euphemism for being educated and having knowledge. The notion of control knowledge has been developed more recently. Thinking, that is, mental work, can now be explained as a complex but understandable process. [2] This increased emphasis on the process of thinking opens up new options for the teaching of intelligence. More and more, it is the process of intelligence, the way we go about evaluating and applying information, that is emphasized. It is the process of thinking that is considered critical. Computer scientists are pointing the way to the study of human intelligence as they try to create "thinking machines." Teachers are placing increasing emphasis on students' awareness of their own thinking skills at all academic levels.

Throughout this book, I emphasize the process of thinking over the product of thinking. This emphasis in no way means that I deny the value of content. The learning of specific content—of a great deal of specific content—is essential preparation for adulthood. But without intelligent processing of that content, it is relatively useless.

EXPERTISE

As members of the modern world, where specialization and focus are appreciated, we have a high regard for expertise. We often speak highly of people who "seem to know a lot" about something. The measurement of book learning or expertise provides a means of designating differences in people's levels of acquired knowledge. We like to rank people (adults and children) this way. [3] Some people are more expert at some things than others. We often mistake this measurement of expertise for an indication of an individual's mental ability.

Expertise is defined by cognitive scientists who study thinking and learning processes as the possession of a body of knowledge including basic facts (such as $2 + 2 = 4$, a cat is a mammal, a hammer is a tool) and various basic procedural information (such as this is how you double a cookie recipe or write a grammatically correct sentence). [4] A student's level of expertise can affect what is called his or her "initial state" or capacity to learn more, to take in and organize—assimilate—new information. [5] This is because incoming information can be connected to information that has been previously stored. In other words, what one already knows determines, at least in part, what one can actually learn. The more you know, the more you can add to what you know. So, *content*—stored information of even the most basic sort—is expertise. Content is essential. Content adds confidence; it provides the person doing the thinking security—a sort of informational blanket. But content is not mental ability.

CONTROL KNOWLEDGE

Control knowledge, the second category of intellectual competence, is more complex than expertise. Control knowledge involves the many ways of coding and distributing knowledge in the brain. [6] It is defined as "knowledge which is directed internally toward the structure of thinking itself." [7] Control knowledge determines when, why, and how other more "material" knowledge (or expertise) is used. [8] In other words, according to Professor Andrea di Sessa, who teaches in the School of Education at the University of California at Berkeley, the value of what and how much one knows, how much content or knowledge one has stored, is determined by how adept one is at controlling or performing more complex mental operations using that knowledge.

Young people should be made aware of the distinction between and the importance of both expertise and control knowledge in intelligent thinking. If your child is under the age of 7, you may choose not to begin teaching your child the scientific terms "expertise" and "control knowledge." You may simply start with discussions about ways of using one's brain. You may want to differentiate between simpler and more complex ways of thinking and then, later on, bring in the scientific terms. I return to this matter in Chapter 10, where I examine the process of learning to learn.

My purpose here is to encourage adults to talk to children about how their minds work, to ask not only "*what* is the answer?" but also "*how* did you get this answer?" To do so, educators and parents must be sensitive to their own and others' common assumptions about thinking and knowing. [9]

COMMON VIEWS REGARDING INTELLIGENCE

We can learn a great deal about how children and adults (ourselves included) view intelligence by asking them. I do this by interviewing people of all ages from all walks of life. I always find an interesting diversity of answers. Let us review a few of these here. I label each of the persons I refer to (my "subjects") with a number so that I can list their ideas for you later. Although my group of subjects is in no way a representative sample of all children and adults, it is a group that teaches us a great deal about the folklore on intelligence. You may find your own views or the views of your child included here somewhere.

Children seem to have, in the main, the sense that intelligence is something that is either learned or practiced (or both) in school. A 3-year-old girl (subject 1) who is perceived as being "very, very bright" by her preschool teachers explains (as if having said it several times before) that "intelligence is that you are articulate and you know your ABC's." A second girl, age 7 (subject 2), claims that intelligence involves "knowing a lot" and "knowing how to get the answers right." Note that both expertise (knowing a lot) and control knowledge (knowing how to get the answers right) are included in her definition. Time and again, I find that competence in problem solving is something that young children recognize, appreciate, and talk about.

A very alert 5-year-old boy (subject 3) is a little more explicit, explaining that being intelligent is "when you know what shapes fit, and *how* to fit them in the right holes, and you can spell words too." In referring to the "how" of fitting shapes into the right holes, he seems to be saying that it is not just what you know, but how you use it. Another perception of intelligence is offered by a contemplative 9-year-old girl (subject 4), who says that intelligence is present in those who can "get the answers faster" and are "good at things in class." Again, a child sees competence as more than just having information. She brings in the element of speed—getting the answers "faster."

The ability to "get" answers is more than simply "knowing a lot," that is, having expertise. Although each of these four children includes the notion that intelligence is what you know (i.e., expertise in the form of knowing ABC's, numbers, etc.), three of them definitely see some element of answer-generating or problem-solving competence in intelligence. These are elements of control knowledge. (We can see here that the term "control knowledge" need not be used in discussing its characteristics. Keep this in mind when you talk to children about intelligence.)

Other more social aspects of intelligence are often found in young people's definitions. The 8-year-old boy (subject 5) who is quoted at the beginning of this chapter also views being "smart" as being able to do "what the teacher wants you to do." This idea suggests itself to be a shrewd mix of compliance and answer getting. Perhaps knowing where and how to be obedient in school is also a form of intelligence.

Two giggling young ladies, ages 15 and 17 (subjects 6 and 7) (who insisted on being interviewed together), go so far as to identify two distinctly different and apparently antagonistic intelligences. The first, "academic intelligence," is not measured on classroom tests but on standardized tests, "when they tell you if you've been studying and learning and if you're gifted or not and stuff like that." The second, "social intelligence," is being able "to handle things well" and "knowing how to act in social situations." This type of intelligence "keeps you from getting embarrassed" and "gets you a lot of friends so you'll fit in."

A third adolescent, a 15-year-old male (subject 8), speaks quite derogatorily about intelligence. For him intelligence is "all mental," has to do "only with school," and is something that "mostly geeks have." Two others, ages 16 and 18 (subjects 9 and 10) (interviewed separately), also see intelligence as being purely academic but not necessarily undesirable. One says "intelligence just happens to you," while the other says "how smart you are depends on how smart your parents are." Here, these young people are hinting at the nature–nurture debate, which I take up in the next chapter.

The notion of "social intelligence" offered by the two girls interviewed together (subjects 6 and 7) actually implies certain types of problem solving, or what we call social control activity, in that it involves "seeing what you want (socially) and figuring out how to get it." The adolescent subjects do note, however, that when social control intelligence is transferred to a high-school physics class, it is not approved of by other students. This form of social control intelligence is described (by subjects 6 and 7) as "kissing up to the teacher" and being a goody-goody or even a "geek" in some cases. Classroom competencies such as teacher pleasing and public showing of answer getting are referred to with negativity by the two adolescents who describe social intelligence. In terms of peer acceptance, some intelligent students may therefore come to feel that it is "smart" to hide their smarts.

Young adults tell us about other aspects of the folklore on intelligence. Two women in their mid-twenties (subjects 11 and 12) explain that intelligence is relative. "If you have street smarts and you don't live in the streets, it doesn't do you any good. Same with cave man abilities. No use these days." One of these subjects (subject 12), a professional cook, thinks that intelligence includes at least three areas of competence and problem solving: "survival, communication, and creativity." According to this young woman, some people are born with these abilities, but anyone can learn them with the right teachers and practice. I find it interesting that these young adults speak positively about street smarts while the adolescents speak negatively about classroom smarts.

A 27-year-old architecture student (subject 13) describes "high intelligence" as a problem-solving capability that depends largely on multidimensional visualization skills. He also includes "the ability to abstract and to symbolize" in his definition of intelligence. Here, the notion that intelligence is a problem-solving capacity is explicitly stated. This subject claims that he understands what he is saying about intelligence because he experiences a high level of these abilities in his own mind. He appears to know control knowledge first hand and to emphasize it over expertise.

A 28-year-old professional artist (subject 14) notes that academic intelligence

> is fine for academics but hasn't helped me much in the real
> world. I'm fortunate that I also have a natural artistic ability
> to earn a living with. It's how I express my ideas, work
> out problems, and support myself. I think that's a kind of
> intelligence—putting complicated ideas into pictures so every-
> one can understand them and then earning a living doing it.

Another young adult, who lost his home and all his possessions in the 1989 California earthquake (subject 15), notes that
being at peace with oneself is intelligent. He says that he was told
repeatedly by a teacher, "If you have any brains you'd listen."
Since then, he has tried to "have brains" and listen very closely.
Being peaceful and quiet and paying very close attention are
attributes of real intelligence, he claims. However, he notes that
there is more to intelligence. He was told by a scientist he met in a
Red Cross shelter that he must have a lot of brains to make it
through the trauma of the earthquake "so together." "Coping
well is also intelligence," he concludes. "It's survival."

People in their thirties offer a wide range of ideas about
intelligence. A 31-year-old computer programmer who is a college dropout but who "went off the top end of the scale on I.Q.
tests all through school" (subject 16) explains that there is a vast
difference between what he terms "potential intelligence," as
measured on I.Q. and aptitude tests, and "actual intelligence,"
which is manifested in the "outer" world. He says,

> I really only respect and believe in actual intelligence. This is a
> high level of understanding, in the day-to-day context, of how
> to apply information to solve problems. If you can't figure out
> how to use your brains in daily life you don't really have any.

In his twenties this respondent had programmed war games for
the U.S. Navy and analyzed MX missile trajectories for a defense
industry corporation.

> I'm glad I'm out of the defense business now. But I learned a lot about how to apply math and statistics and science to real-life problems in that work. No one really showed me this in school. I was too intelligent to go to college. Education really misses the mark. But now people think I'm slow because I don't have a B.A.

A 35-year-old businesswoman (subject 17) claims that intelligence is simply curiosity. "The more curious you are, the more intelligent you are. That is all I have to say." She was not interested in continuing the conversation or at all curious about what others may have said about the subject.

A 37-year-old ranch manager who, in his words, "never bothered to go to college" (subject 18) explains that "intelligent people really listen to what I have to say. They are open to new input. They are able to learn new ways of understanding the world. They are not stuck."

A 38-year-old chiropractic student (quoted at the beginning of this chapter) (subject 19) who grew up "on the really poor side of town" recalls learning that being intelligent was finding a way out of poverty.

> Thank God I was smart enough to do that. But now I think intelligence is only intelligence if a person brings information in from many avenues. One kind of information getting alone is not intelligent. You have to see things from many angles, not linearly. I'm glad I've been going to school. It's making me learn a new way of seeing things. I can combine this way with my old ways of knowing. This is power. I'm ending up with a lot more than people who didn't come up my way.

A 37-year-old professor (subject 20) tries to tell me what he thinks intelligence is. After five minutes of beginning sentences and breaking off in the middle of them, he apologizes. "I'm sorry. This is the first time I've realized that I have no idea what intelligence really is. It's an overwhelming question. Does this mean I'm not intelligent?" He laughs nervously.

I encounter considerations of a more philosophical tone among subjects in their forties. One subject, a woman who loves animals (subject 21), explains that

> intelligence is supposed to help a species survive. If we humans are so intelligent, how come we're destroying our ecosystem and threatening our own lives? People forget about animal intelligence. Humans have somehow evolved what they call "intelligent thought." Thought has become so important that we don't trust our senses the way animals do anymore.

She feels that what humans call intelligence is merely one form of human thought, a form with which she is not very impressed.

Another subject, whose mother is a Native American (subject 22), holds similar views, with an added spiritual element. "Intelligence is trusting your intuitions and having refined intuitions to trust. We get this trained out of us in school. We lose touch with what we really need to know." She also explains that one's intelligence increases as one gains the ability to see things from many different perspectives.

> This is the lesson of the medicine wheel. You put something in a big circle you make on the ground. Everyone around the circle sees the same thing differently, from a different angle. In life you have to know where you are in the circle and you have to try to gain as many different perspectives as possible on the same thing. I think that the more you do this, the more intelligent you are.

A 46-year-old businessman (subject 23) tells me that intelligence is "thinking clearly and precisely." It is also "mental organization" and "the ability to tackle problems without getting emotional." He goes on to explain that "many people get emotional or give up on problems, even numerical problems, because they don't have any confidence in their ability to think things through step by step."

A 45-year-old taxi driver (subject 24) claims that "some

people are just born stupid. I can find my way around any city. If you give me a few days, I practically memorize the map. I can see it in my head. That's intelligent."

A 42-year-old mother of three (subject 25) tells me that her oldest child is the most intelligent in school, "But I like to think that each of my kids is intelligent in a different way. No one can have all the intelligences at once." She also notes that intelligence in school is the ability to solve the problems the teachers assign, and that "this kind of thinking may not really be useful later on in life."

As people get older, they may or may not add to their definitions of intelligence. A female administrator in her early fifties (subject 26) tells me that intelligence is evidenced by how quickly a person can think. A 53-year-old psychologist (subject 27) remarks that intelligence is being able to make "conceptual leaps" from one level of knowledge to a higher level of knowledge in the same domain, or across domains. Another respondent in her mid-fifties (subject 28) comments that intelligence is "using words and numbers well, remembering things and using what you know." One gentleman (subject 29) tells me that "there's no such thing as intelligence. It's only a figment of our imagination. But you have to be pretty sharp to imagine that it exists and what it's like."

A 50-year-old entrepreneur (subject 30) wants to know my "operational definition of intelligence" before answering my question. When he is told that I have none to offer him, he says he will create his own. "But first," he says, "if you want to know if someone is intelligent, ask him." Then he gives me what he calls his operational definition: "(1) having total recall; (2) cross-talk amongst the categories of information stored in the brain; (3) making jumps to new conceptualizations based on that cross-talk; (4) thinking in four or five dimensions at once; (5) doing all of the above very quickly." He then concludes that although he can imagine what it is like to have an intelligent brain, he is not very intelligent.

I interviewed a 63-year-old who was a retired "Documentation Department Manager" from a major defense industry corporation (subject 31). His work had involved translating highly complex operations, such as those involved in running nuclear submarines, into a language that enlistees in the Navy could understand and creating operations manuals for such purposes. He says that he takes a long time to decide whether someone is intelligent or not. He lists these "elements of intelligence": (1) An intelligent person is one who "knows a lot about the world—has a very comprehensive knowledge"; (2) He or she also "has increasingly better ways to put things into perspective"; (3) "The mark of intelligence is that it be always leading toward a higher state of being—being able to cope with yourself and the world in an evermore noble fashion"; and (4) "A lot of hard work is involved in becoming intelligent."

A 68-year-old man (subject 32) offers yet another view of intelligence. "Intelligence is mindfulness. Mindfulness involves really noticing what the object is, staying intensely aware and in the present moment. As mindfulness and concentration get stronger, the mind becomes more powerful, more keenly aware, more insightful, more intelligent." [10] According to this man, expertise and control knowledge are part of the thought process. They are appropriate at times; however, they are not really higher intelligence. They are not steps toward the true "mindfulness" of the highest intelligence. Yet his conscious application of mindfulness is, in effect, a high level of control knowledge (such as the consciousness technology described in Chapter 12).

WHAT THE FOLKLORE
ON INTELLIGENCE TELLS US

Let us summarize these ideas about intelligence. It is obvious that a multitude of fascinating notions about intelligence exist.

Many, but not all, people's assumptions regarding intelligence are intuitively related to the concepts of expertise and control knowledge. I have charted these related concepts in the following pages. I have listed any notion that in some way might be viewed as suggesting that expertise or control knowledge is involved in intelligence. I had to stretch these concepts for children's replies (e.g., interpreting "knowing the ABC's" as a form of expertise). For that matter, I had to do the same for many of the adults. Note that many of the notions listed are starred. The more stars I award a particular notion, the closer it comes to the definitions of expertise and control knowledge I offer at the beginning of this chapter.

Sub- ject	Age	Expertise	Control	Other
1	3	Know ABC's★★	Are articulate	
2	7	Know a lot★★★	Know how to get answers right★★★	
3	8	Know what shapes fit★★, able to spell★★	Know how to fit the shapes	
4	9	Good at things in class★★	Get answers faster★★★	
5	5	—	Do what the teacher wants★	
6	15	Academic intelligence	Social control intelligence★	Social intelligence
7	17	Academic intelligence	Social control intelligence★	Social intelligence
8	15	Academic intelligence	All mental	

(*continued*)

Sub-ject	Age	Expertise	Control	Other
9	16	Academic intelligence	Academic intelligence	
10	18	Academic intelligence	Academic intelligence	
11	Mid 20s	Intelligence is relative★	Abilities which can be used★★★	Street smarts if you live in the streets
12	Mid 20s	Intelligence is relative	Survival, communication, and crea-tivity★★★	Creativity
13	27	—	Multidimensional visualization, ability to abstract and symbolize	
14	28	Relevant expertise must be useful in real world★★★	Putting complicated ideas into pictures	
15	Mid 20s	—	Paying attention, being quiet, listening closely, coping★★	Coping
16	31	—	Actual intelligence is ability to apply knowledge★★★	
17	35	—		Curiosity★★
18	37	—	Really listening, ability to learn new ways★★	
19	38	—	Using multiple avenues★★★	

(*continued*)

Sub-ject	Age	Expertise	Control	Other
20	37	—	—	
21	Mid 40s	—	Intelligence should help a species survive	
22	Mid 40s	—	Using intuitions★★★, seeing things from multiple perspectives★★★★	
23	46	—	Mental organ-ization★★★, step-by-step thinking, think-ing clearly and precisely★★★★	
24	45	—	Spatial memory, i.e., memorizing a map★★★★	
25	42	—	Ability to solve problems teachers assign★★★	
26	Early 50s	—	How quickly one can think★★	
27	53	—	Ability to make conceptual leaps★★★★	
28	Mid 50s	—	Using words and numbers well★★★, remembering things very well★★★★	

(*continued*)

Sub-ject	Age	Expertise	Control	Other
29	50s	—	Being able to imagine what intelligence is	
30	50	—	Total recall★★★, cross–talk★★★★★, conceptual jumps★★★★★, thinking in many dimensions at once★★★★★, doing all this quickly★★★★★	
31	63	Very comprehensive knowl-edge★★★★★, a lot of hard work★★★★	Ability to put things into per-spective★★★★★, leading to higher state of being★★★, improved coping★★★	
32	68	Useful but not intelligence	Mindfulness, controlling one's awareness of the present moment	Mindfulness, being very aware of the present moment

During these interviews, I observed that:

- All but one of my subjects appeared confident about their definitions of intelligence.
- Of my subjects over the age of 20, most were able to *explain*, at least briefly, their theories regarding intelligence.

- About one third of my subjects elaborated on their definitions of intelligence enough that I could detect distinct components in their definitions.
- Many of my subjects described a component of intelligence that in some way could be interpreted as expertise.
- Most of my subjects described a component of intelligence that in some way could be interpreted as some form of control knowledge.

Consider some of their ideas about intelligence that suggest an awareness of control knowledge:

Intelligence involves knowing *how* to use material knowledge:

Subject 2—Knowing how to get answers right
Subject 3—Knowing *how* to fit the shapes
Subject 28—Using words and numbers *well*

Intelligence involves being adept at *controlling or performing mental operations* on material knowledge:

Subject 25—Having the ability to solve problems
Subject 13—Using multidimensional visualization
             Having the ability to abstract and symbolize
Subject 22—Seeing things from multiple perspectives
Subject 23—Step-by-step thinking
             Thinking clearly and precisely
Subject 27—Having the ability to make conceptual leaps
Subject 30—Having cross-talk ability
             Thinking in many dimensions at once
Subject 31—Having the ability to put things into perspective

EMPHASIS ON CONTROL KNOWLEDGE

I am especially intrigued by the response of subject 31, who says that, "It takes a lot of hard work to be intelligent." This perception of intelligence as something the individual can attain through hard work suggests that there are or can be degrees of self-consciousness and self-determination in intelligence. My own belief is that to work hard to be intelligent involves knowing what kind of hard work will produce or enhance what kind of intelligence. If one can clarify for oneself what intelligence is, perhaps one can also clarify for oneself how to go about getting it. And this is what parents must do in their own minds when they decide to help develop their children's intelligence. They must clarify for themselves the meaning of or the various meanings of intelligence. This must be an ongoing process, as both children and adults can learn more about how their minds work over time. Parents must also set up clear routes to acquiring the desired intelligences.

Control knowledge—knowing how to think—is an essential intelligence. The replies of twenty-six of the thirty-two people I quote in this chapter suggest to me that many people have a sense that something which is or which can be interpreted as being control knowledge is a component of intelligence. Many quite appropriately understand control knowledge to be a mental process exercised upon expertise or "material" knowledge.

Much of this book focuses on the development of control knowledge and on the factors that support the development of control knowledge, such as self-esteem, an understanding of the purpose of struggle, family support, concentration, brain capacity, and a stimulating collection of early experiences. It is in the development of control knowledge that learning to learn, learning to think, and learning to use information intelligently are ensured. Because control knowledge is more subtle, more complex, and perhaps more fragile than expertise, it is important to emphasize the means of developing such knowledge or intelligence. Above all, it is important that educators, parents, and children become increasingly aware of control knowledge and its applications. This increasing awareness can become part of the new folklore on intelligence. It can become part of your ongoing conversations with the young people in your life.

Chapter 3

Scientific Definitions of Intelligence and the Freedom of Thought

A lively and impudent gnat was daring enough to attack a lion, whom he so enraged by stinging the most sensitive parts of his nose, eyes and ears that the beast roared in anguish . . .

The gnat, hovering over the spot, and sounding a trumpet note of triumph, happened to come in the way of the delicate web of a spider. Slight as it was, it was enough to stop him. His efforts to escape only fixed him more firmly in the toils, and he who had vanquished the lion became the prey of the spider.

—The Lion and the Gnat
in C. Colladi's *Aesop's Fables*

The notion that human intelligence can be learned or acquired has become especially controversial in recent decades. Pressures to provide educational opportunities for all of America's youths have forced lawmakers, educators, and parents to examine their beliefs regarding the learnability of intelligence. Many believe, or claim to believe, that intelligence can be learned: If intelligence is influenced by socioeconomic environment, then improving the environment should raise intelligence. Moreover, providing all children "the right" educational stimulation should improve the mental performance of all of them. Others argue that these theories and beliefs are incorrect, that intelligence cannot be learned.

Although the division lines have long been drawn, education still plays on a field of doubt regarding the source of mental ability. Although we tend to assume that our schools' educational programs and policies are based on undisputed facts, they are, at the deepest level, driven by belief systems and theories. The very existence of educational institutions is based on the belief that something can be learned in school—that school can teach factual matter as well as thinking processes, expertise as well as control knowledge. Parents must recognize the tensions affecting their own and their children's teachers' efforts or lack of efforts to raise their children's mental ability. I have included this chapter in order to explain some of these tensions. Some of the concepts I discuss are complex and theoretical. I suggest that you read this chapter when you have the time to consider the way these concepts can be related to your own views.

THE NATURE–NURTURE DEBATE

The educator seeks to *interact with* rather than *act upon* the student's mind; the mind never arrives in the classroom as a blank slate. Were it to do so, education would be a very different task.

Let us briefly consider an impossible science-fiction scenario: Assume for a moment that, through some feat of genetic engineering, we have rendered the population of students as blank slates. Somehow, they all arrive in their first classrooms this way. Students sit, perhaps motionless and robotically obedient, like automatons awaiting curricular programming. Educators recite, demonstrate, or otherwise relay information to students. Students mentally absorb this information, filling their once-blank mental slates. The entire educational process is condensed into a brief chunk of time. Getting educated resembles being inoculated. The student's mind, analogous to the computer, goes in for an injection of programming and a series of data bank installations.

Assume that this futuristic process serves as the guarantor of an eerie form of social equality. As long as every student arrives as a blank slate and is fed the same program and the same data, every student knows the same thing, shares the same biases, and has the same abilities. The opportunities for programming and thus control of the masses abound. The state mandates that nothing be taught that might enable students to question or to see alternative viewpoints. All officially approved, controlled information is distributed equally. Every student is of the same mind, having learned the same thing. Later in life, when uniformity of thought has been ensured in their generation, students are randomly tracked into a higher education aimed at specific training to fill occupational quotas. Still, their uniform mental foundations prevail.

But then, an unexpected dose of radiation causes a series of genetic mutations, generating some differences in the mental hardware belonging to some of the next generation of students. All students continue to arrive in school with their blank mental slates, but some of their slates are now larger, more efficient, faster, have more storage space, and have more cross-filing capability than others. The student automatons begin to evidence their individual differences in their learning processes. Educators begin to struggle with these differences. Random tracking of students into specific higher-education training is difficult to maintain or to justify now.

Somehow our imaginary educators decide, quite incorrectly, that all slates are created blank but some are created blanker than others. The scientists begin to fight amongst themselves as to whether or not a nurturing education will improve the capabilities of the blanker slates. They even argue endlessly about whether or not nurture can override nature and whether or not nature has any bearing at all on the outcome of education. Without knowing the answer, educators try an array of curricular designs. The students' minds are the handy subjects of a massive and very naive social experiment, an experiment almost too large for them to recognize.

In our world today, educational programs, along with many other social programs and policies, conduct similarly naive experiments. The modern nature–nurture, that is, inherited-versus-acquired-intelligence, debate [1] and its various hypotheses emerge, at least in part, from an older philosophical question: Can intelligence exist in the mind apart from environmental stimulation or is it basically acquired and derived from the environment by the senses? Can the circle or the triangle (or any concept) exist in the mind without sensory input, or can it only arrive there by way of sensory data drawn from the environment? Is the mind, without input from its environment, empty—merely a blank slate, tablet, or vessel that contains nothing, waiting to be filled?

This age-old philosophical debate is really quite simple. On one side of the argument, philosophical *rationalists* believe that reasoning—thought—exists in the mind regardless of environmental stimulation. The rationalist would tell you that logical processes are basic to the mind and not learned from the environment. The mind imposes its inherent powers of reasoning upon any and all incoming sensory experience. The mind is best suited to know when it relies upon its internal reasoning processes rather than on sensory data from the environment. Philosophical *empiricists*, on the other side of the argument, believe that to "know" anything is to draw information from the environment; to know is to have a good foundation of externally induced sensory impressions. There is no knowledge without full use of these impressions. The empiricist would tell you that you learn to think from the world around you.

Although various mixes of rationalism and empiricism have emerged over time, they have not diffused the essential conflict between these two diametrically opposed views.

SCIENCE AND INTELLIGENCE

Modern science has transformed what was once a philosophical conflict into what appears to be conflicting facts. On the one hand, intelligence may be largely determined by genetic code. Such a position is supported by results of numerous studies of adopted children that show that the I.Q.'s of children who are adopted at birth are much closer to the I.Q.'s of their biological siblings and parents than to those of their adopted siblings and parents. [2] This suggests that biological (genetically inherited) factors influence intelligence more powerfully than environmental (adopted family) factors. Studies of fraternal and identical twins support this view. The I.Q.'s of twins who are separated at birth become increasingly similar as the twins develop, with the most powerful similarities being between identical twins, who share identical genetic material. [3] The stronger the genetic resemblance, the higher the correlation. These findings suggest that genetic makeup is a powerful determinant of intelligence and that it explains much of the variation in individual intelligence. [4]

On the other hand, intelligence may be so extensively influenced by environment that we cannot detect the actual intensity of this influence. The influence of environment upon intelligence may extend across the generations through the centuries. The authors of *Not in Our Genes*, R. C. Lewontin, Steven Rose, and Leon Kamin, suggest that perhaps we are applying the wrong level of analysis to our nature–nurture debate. [5] This line of argument says that biological determinists, those who believe that genes determine mental ability—that intelligence is inherited— are unwittingly (and sometimes not so unwittingly) preserving inequality in society. [6] The argument also says that biology is not the primary determinant of mental ability. Subjective labeling can be arbitrary and detrimental. It can also work the other way. It is therefore very important to examine carefully labels given children regarding their levels of mental ability. It has been suggested that children's low I.Q. scores can be improved just by telling their teachers that these children are late developers. [7] The effects of I.Q. and intelligence labeling are implicit but pervasive: Labeling preserves a social order in which some children are guaranteed access to the higher echelons of ability and power by being born into the middle and upper classes. [8]

So how do we weed through the jungle of this debate? Well, one answer to this question is that we do not. We skip the debate. Why argue about the *possibility* that intelligence is inherited? Let us instead shift our focus to the *expression* of intelligence, regardless of its origin. The expression of intelligence can be taught and encouraged. It can also be neglected and obliterated. And it often is.

INTELLIGENCE ON THE SCIENTIFIC FRONTIER

At this point, it is important to talk about "cognitive science." Cognitive science owes much of its development to the development of the modern computer. [9] Some cognitive scientists maintain that something called *mental representation* is done by the mind. This mental representation is best described as higher-order thinking—thinking about thinking, control-level thinking [10], or what we can call *metacognitive activity*. Metacognitive science suggests that a mental suprastructure exists within the mind, that the mind watches itself work and directs itself as it works.

Professor Howard Gardner explains that "Where forty years ago few scientists dared to speak of schemas, images, rules, transformations, and other mental structures and operations, these representational assumptions and concepts are now taken for granted." [11] Cognitive science thus opens the door to new (or the reasking of old) questions about the mind. Science offers increasing evidence of the links between psychological, computational, and neurological processes. In light of the evidence that in our heads we house a powerful biocomputer [12], the brain is more readily accepted as being the originator and director of mental activity and of the mental structures that organize and operate upon that activity.

For some, this new scientific view of the brain supports the old rationalist explanation of mental activity: Perhaps the brain *is* complex enough to give rise to thoughts from within itself, after all. If the complexity of the brain is inherited, and if this complexity affects the intelligence of the individual who inherits it, then intelligence may be quite affected by genetic makeup. [13]

But most cognitive scientists no longer "care" whether the rationalists or the empiricists "win" the old debate. [14] Cognitive scientists find the mental representations, or *cognitive schemata*, to be so very important in themselves that notions regarding their ultimate origin take a back seat. Mental ability can arise wherever it does, but once it exists, it is important to handle it well.

THE NEW QUESTIONS

Cognitive science might succeed in officially moving us well beyond the old struggle between rationalism and empiricism; however, this same struggle threatens to continue and to retard progress in our management of children's education. Until we believe that much more can be done to realize children's mental potentials, we will do little more to realize these potentials.

If a parent, or a teacher or a school or a textbook author, assumes that he or she can have a great deal of influence on the expression of a child's mental ability, then an effort will be made to exert this influence. The more we all know about how to enhance the expression of mental ability, the more we will seek to do so and the more effective our efforts will be.

FREEDOM OF THOUGHT

The institution of education prepares the mind to fit into the encompassing social system. In support of this essential process, countless textbooks, lesson plans, and curricula have been developed. We must, however, be continually mindful of the risk inherent in our institutionalized process of mental training (the process we choose to call "education"). We risk teaching that everyone should think in about the same way. Institutionalized mental training or schooling risks encouraging the homogenization of intellectual activity, or, at least, it favors an acceptable range of intellectual activity within the society. In the face of this institutional pressure toward sameness, the preservation of intellectual diversity is critical. A single standard for, or definition of, intelligence may therefore be quite dangerous.

Proponents of both sides of the nature–nurture conflict are missing the point. While the debate has waged on in all its convolutions, we have overlooked the ultimate question: Is the diversity of intellectual activity, and even of free thought, becoming archaic—an anachronism? Is it slipping away in the fashion that grains of sand leave a hand, imperceptibly until enough is gone for an observer finally to notice the difference? As intellectual diversity and thus free thought leave our grasps, are we increasingly unaware of their loss?

The connection between freedom of thought and the development of children's intelligence is a complex one. This connection is at once painfully subtle and grossly concrete. It is made on the many levels of biological and social organization in which we live. Intelligence is difficult to define without inferring that it is either largely biologically or largely environmentally determined. Although freedom of thought is determined by social and political forces, it can be empowered by a diversity of intelligences. Social recognition of a diversity of intelligences allows for diversity of thought.

The dangerous concept that all human intelligence resides on a single scale from low to high implies that some very similarly thinking members of the population have higher degrees of mental competence than do others. A societal preference for or recognition of such a single scale of intelligence suggests that only the thought processes that measure high on that particular scale are intelligent thought processes.

Perhaps the educational system exists to organize children—and all citizens—along a continuum of intellect, one that contains the highest potential of a particular intelligence at one end and lesser degrees of that same intelligence down the line. If so, then we as a society are selecting and favoring the thought processes best serving that continuum. People who think, and who, to a smaller or larger degree, express their intelligences differently, may actually be thinking according to a different intellectual model that exists on a separate scale. They will, nevertheless, be organized along the official scale. Freedom to think differently—to apply alternate intellectual strategies and to engage in free thinking itself—can become viewed as alien to the social order. Alternative and very valuable forms of intelligence can go unrecognized, unselected, unexpressed. And then they can atrophy, suffocate, and die off.

Chapter 4

Modern Education
and Intelligence

i wish a star
could go so
far i could
touch one
or more

EBM

> "There's no use trying," (Alice) said: "one *can't* believe impossible things."
>
> "I daresay you haven't had much practice," said the Queen. "When I was your age, I always did it for half-an-hour a day. Why, sometimes I've believed as many as six impossible things before breakfast . . ."
>
> —Alice and the Queen conversing in
> Lewis Carroll's *Through the Looking Glass*

Teachers express as many different views of intelligence as the rest of us. They frequently emphasize the notion that there are many different types of intelligence or mental ability and that no one student has a corner on the market of "smarts": "Every child is special" and "Most children will excel at something if given the opportunity" are frequently heard teachers' comments.

Although most modern teachers express such egalitarian, democratic views regarding their students' abilities, they are under pressure to favor certain types of students in their classrooms. We can explain this if we think in terms of an economy of attention: there is only so much to go around. Supply will never meet demand. When faced with what can range from fifteen to forty students, the students most difficult to teach or to control may get more disciplinary and corrective attention than others. However, the more cooperative, attentive, responsive students are the most likely to be positively acknowledged and to be considered "good" students. Although a "good student" and an "intelligent child" may not always be one and the same, the good student is usually regarded as the relatively intelligent child. A child paying attention in class, completing assignments, and getting good grades appears to be smart enough to do this. So, in terms of academic intelligence (defined by subjects 9 and 10, in Chapter 2), this child is intelligent. Teacher pleasing is "smart."

Although teachers tend to believe that the child's environment has a profound effect upon that child's expression of academic intelligence and general mental ability, teachers do not hold the classroom environment entirely, or even primarily, responsible for that expression. I often hear teachers explain that they feel unsupported by families: parents do not help with homework, parents do not emphasize the importance of school, parents do not get involved in school activities, parents do not teach their children to pay attention, parents do not teach their children manners and acceptable behaviors, parents send their children to school hungry, or sleepy and needing a nap. Yes, parents are guilty as charged—of some of these behaviors some of the time. But parental behavior does not explain entirely children's failure to show mental ability. Some mix of parenting, teaching, playing, watching television, and other factors is responsible.

Teachers, quite rightly, want off the hot seat. So do parents. And this is not surprising: educating children is actually a team effort. Encouraging children to develop and express their intelligences is also a team effort. One of the outcomes of this team effort is the child's academic performance. Academic performance and intelligence are spoken of almost synonymously. This should alert us to the impact of the team effort on the child's expression of intelligence in the classroom.

HOW DO TEACHERS SPOT "INTELLIGENT CHILDREN"?

Teachers see some of their children completing their assignments more rapidly and more correctly than the rest. These children tend to be more attentive in class and to ask the most appropriate questions. "Of course," a fourth-grade teacher explained to me, "there is always the bright child without the confidence or the social skills necessary for school success. But those kids are the exception, not the rule."

During my many conversations with school teachers over the years, I have heard certain characteristics used to define intelligent children most frequently. These characteristics include general curiosity, focused inquisitiveness, continuing interest, and a high degree of alertness. An inner-city schoolteacher claimed, "The curious students want to know, they want to learn." A seventh-grade teacher at a parochial school told me that she could always pick out the intelligent students on the first day of school. "I spot them, that's all. They are interested; they are intelligent." A science teacher in Ohio reported, "I just catch a look of curiosity in the student's eye. . . . I wait for, I live for, that look. Then I know I've hooked the kid. Then I know I'm really teaching someone, that I've found someone who can really learn." A kindergarten teacher in California said, "Bright kids are awake. . . . Or, if not, they can be woken up. When I spot 'em, I wake 'em up and then I don't let 'em go."

BEING "SPOTTED" AS "AVERAGE"

What happens when children are not identified as being intelligent? They are usually identified as being average and then treated as such. Several effects result from being labeled "average":

- Teachers' and school administrators' expectations are that the child will perform at a consistently average level.
- The child, receiving few prompts to exceed this level, performs at the acceptable level of average.
- The child comes to view himself or herself as average and seeks to maintain no higher than a consistently average performance.

- The parents either express a desire for the child to exceed the demands of being average or accept the child's average academic performance and even reward it.

The last point warrants more discussion. Whenever parents of a child who has come to be identified as an average student demand more than average academic performance of that child, the child will do some combination of the following:

- Meet the parents' demands.
- Feel conflicted in experiencing conflicting sets of demands (excellent versus average performance).
- Feel no conflict in continuing to perform in an average way at school where a critical mass of teachers, fellow students, and even the child all perceive that child as being average.

Being spotted as average can be a very convincing experience for the child. But "average" is an artifact; it is an invented reality. No one is average. Yet, sadly, most schoolchildren have come to believe that they are average. This is not surprising since somebody has to be "average." In fact, most people have to be about average to make average the average.

THE PROBLEM OF EDUCATIONAL TRACKING

Sometimes children are labeled as "below average." As damning as being labeled average can be, being labeled below average is even more serious. I have seen children who are actually of average and, sometimes, of above-average mental ability labeled as "below average" and even as "retarded." After a certain number of years of being told that one is mentally slow, and being taught only that which can be learned by someone who is mentally slow, one begins to assume the characteristics of someone who is mentally slow. Whether a child is formally placed with other children who are also labeled below average or informally grouped with these children, the label becomes part of the child's self-perception.

What happens very early in a child's school career can determine the course of that child's life. Once a child is placed on the "slow" or the "average" track, the child tends to stay there. Children placed on the "fast" track may stay there throughout school or only until puberty, when other factors can come into play.

Once a child is assigned to a track, his or her reading, math, science, and other lessons are given at that level. Imagine that a bright child ends up spending three years learning math at what is for him an unchallenging, average pace. That child will, most likely, have a difficult time moving up to the challenging fast track in math the next school year. The experiential gap is now too big. The children who have been moving at a rapid pace are further along in the content of the math lessons. Over the years, the gap has grown.

Gifted, exceptionally bright, or exceptionally talented children are also affected by being labeled. We as a society are divided about the meaning and the importance of giftedness. Different school districts handle what they call "gifted" children in different ways. And within school districts and schools, children are treated inequitably, often causing discomfort to children who have been labeled as gifted as well as to those who have not.

Many gifted children experience the discomfort of being treated differently throughout their school years. Receiving the label of "gifted," which sounds as if it should be a blessing, can be a burden. A female college freshman told me that she was called "the school brain" in junior high and high school and was teased and ostracized for being one. She was "plagued by the label for years" and eventually decided to, in her own words, "suppress my intelligence and reduce my vocabulary in order to have more friends." Whether the label of "gifted" or "brain" is accurately or mistakenly applied, it can hurt.

But not receiving the label can be at least as detrimental as receiving it. There are many gifted children out there who no one has noticed and who receive no special education whatsoever. Parents must know about the various gifted programs available to their children and how children are selected for participation.

GIFTED PROGRAMS

Gifted programs take a variety of forms. And parents, teachers, and professionals have a variety of feelings about these forms. Some programs for gifted children emphasize academics and others focus on adjustment, isolation, and other psychological issues. There is a lot of disagreement about which is more important. Gifted programs can be regular classroom programs, special individualized programs, "cluster programs," or "pull-out" programs. They can be special weekly or daily classes or entire special schools. Programs that involve more classroom time are not always better programs. Sometimes children who are called "gifted" become separated from other children in ways that fool them about life or stigmatize them. Quite naturally, schools tend to select the gifted programs that are least costly or that fit into their budgets more readily.

Services for gifted children usually take the form of either acceleration, enrichment, special grouping, or guidance. In brief, these are:

- *Acceleration*: the advancement of a student in the sequence of elementary and secondary years of school by way of early admission to grade school or college; the skipping and/or combining of grades and other amendments to the standard program. Acceleration is the least costly form of gifted education because no additional programs are required.

- *Enrichment*: the adaptation of a program to serve the gifted via the addition of special areas of learning and/or learning experiences to the standard curriculum.
- *Special grouping*: the placing together of gifted students to learn at an advanced pace and to motivate and stimulate one another, for all or a portion of the school week.
- *Guidance*: the provision of special counseling to gifted students and sometimes to their families, addressing the individual and interpersonal needs typical of gifted youth. This counseling looks at social ostracism, boredom, wanting to be accepted by peers, pressure to be outstanding, conceit, isolation, and family relationships. Counseling and guidance focus on what we call "affective" development. This may be as important as or more important than educational efforts, because emotional well-being has a lot to do with the ability to learn.

As indicated earlier, budgetary as well as organizational problems affect the characteristics of gifted programs. At the elementary level, special pull-out programs tend to cost more per student than full-time, self-contained gifted education classes. Special seminars at the secondary level tend to cost more per student than grouping by subject at the secondary level. This is because, in the latter cases, students merely exchange one class for another, and the school system does not need to develop a special structure to provide gifted education.

Whether one child is more gifted than another is not the question. Some children just happen to be in the right school or school district at the right time. One of the terrific conflicts for educators and psychologists who conduct and use results of intelligence tests to place children in gifted programs is the definition of intelligence. The jury is not only still out, it is quite hung on the matter.

HOW THE EDUCATIONAL SYSTEM SEALS A CHILD'S FATE

It is usually nine years from the time a child enters kindergarten to that child's graduation from eighth grade. During these critical formative years, a child is identified as being of below-average, average, or above-average academic ability. That child is deemed cooperative and compliant, or withdrawn, or trouble causing. He or she has been either intentionally or inadvertently labeled. This labeling, or framing, as per performance in school, molds the child's definition of himself or herself.

This is not surprising. Children spend on average five days of the week at school and, on those days, about half of their waking hours at school. A good portion of the remainder of waking hours on school days is filled with school-related activities: dressing for school, doing homework, participating in formal afterschool activities, and associating with (playing with, talking to, and telephoning) schoolmates. Children's selection of school friends tends to organize around the identification of students with similar social or academic characteristics. Because so many of the characteristics are labeled at school, school defines most children's social lives. In these ways, school, as much as, or more than, family, exerts a powerful molding influence upon a young person's identity.

This power is an integral part of the socialization process. School is the institution that prepares children for participation in society (as consumers, parents, voters, and labor-force participants). Because the machinery of school is so massive, so far reaching, parents find themselves feeling increasingly powerless in the determination of their children's characters as their children move through the school years. While, at first, in the kindergarten and first-grade years, there seems to be a balance between school and family, or even a preservation of the power of family over that of outside institutions including school, by second grade many parents report that school life seems to have more influence over their children than family life: "I've lost control over him. He listens to his teacher much more than to me." "If I need to discipline the kid, I hope the school does first. They're more effective down there." Perhaps this is how it should be. I do not express a bias in either direction here. However, I do contend that no matter how busy they are earning a living and managing a home, parents must make every effort to remain on the front line of their children's development, especially from kindergarten through eighth grade. They can share that frontline position with teachers, ministers, rabbis, soccer coaches, and others in any proportion they choose. But parents must not withdraw.

The key reason for not withdrawing is that our children need defense against institutions. This means that in a society with a large population and many large bureaucracies, no matter how humanely we feel children (and adults) should be treated, there is the tendency to treat people like numbers. We are all pieces of a large machine. A child may therefore receive special attention and care at school, but that child is still one of many children, just one of "the kids in line," most of whom are unrelated to each other and to the teachers and most of whom will spend no more than one school year in close contact with any given teacher. And quite often, our children do not receive special attention and care at school. Instead, they become invisible pieces of a mass. Parents must constantly watch the effect of school on their children. Again, this watching is essential, even when a parent is very pleased with the child's teacher, classroom, classmates, and school.

How can parents keep an eye on the effects of schooling—of institutionalization—on their children? Parents must make every effort to:

- *Visit the classroom at least a few times during the year.* If an unannounced visit is considered inappropriate at your child's school, then schedule visits. As your child gets older, be aware that this might embarrass him or her. Discuss the likelihood of your visit with your adolescent-age child beforehand.
- *Be a present parent.* Drive on field trips or attend class or team events. Make your name and face part of the scene. Even if you are an employed parent (which most of us are), be willing to use sick time, floating holidays, vacation days, or exchanged work hours to be at the school at least once a month.
- *Attend all parent–teacher conferences.* This is the only official time to discuss your child's school performance with the teacher, unless your child gets into trouble—and why wait for that?

Parents must watch for early indications of maladjustment to school in their children:

- *Note excessive complaints about school.* Careful on this one. Most children complain about some aspects of school at some times. What we are looking for here is an ongoing and profoundly negative view of school and everything about it.
- *Watch children who feign sickness.* When these children actually miss an unusual amount of school, they may be indicating attitude problems. However, be certain that your child has a full medical checkup before ruling out physical health problems (see Chapter 6 for more on this).
- *Examine unexplained tardiness and absences.* Children who, without their parents' knowledge, do not arrive at school on time, do not make it to particular classes, or do not make it to school at all are asking for someone to notice their trouble complying with the rules.

- *Follow up on reports of misbehavior.* Antisocial, aggressive, and inappropriate behaviors at school are, of course, a call for parent–teacher communication.
- *Pay attention to consistently low grades.* These are indicative of a problem. While attitude problems may be the reason for low grades, it is best for parents to hold back their punishments and instead seek information regarding the child's perception of his or her own learning abilities.

Especially in the early years of elementary school, teachers tend to be quite sensitive to the potentially devastating effects of the transition from home to school. (This transition is elaborated on in Chapter 6.) Specific efforts can be made by teachers in these areas:

- *Define and discuss the difficulty in transition* that children are having. Telling them that this happens to some children and that it will get easier is soothing.
- *Set aside a certain number of minutes of class time*, first thing in the morning, for "phasing in" to the classroom environment.
- *Discuss the issue with parents* in newsletters and conferences.

THE PLIGHT OF EDUCATORS

It is all too easy for us to expect teachers to do more and better work with our children. We do best to remind ourselves that teachers' work is some of the most important and most ambitious work ever done. Teachers teach children; they build an educational foundation of bedrock. Our society depends on teachers to prepare our children for the future, to ensure the future.

Society has become increasingly dependent on schoolteachers because parents, especially mothers, have less and less time with their own children. As a working parent confessed,

"I'm so glad my son has an affectionate teacher. At least he gets some love somewhere. God knows, I can hardly keep things together let alone find time for him anymore." Twenty years ago, most schoolchildren came from two-parent families. Many of them had a stay-home parent who was (at least in principle) available to help them with their growing pains—at home. Those parents, when concerned about what they could do to help their children's education, may have had more time to focus on the matter.

If families with two working parents are stretched to their limits, what of single-parent families? Nowadays, one-third to one-half of schoolchildren come from families broken by divorce. This means that in many geographic areas, 50 percent of all children live with one parent and that about half of today's children have had their lives severely disrupted. They come to school with new problems and new needs and often without having had parental supervision of their schoolwork. Their single parents are so busy "keeping it together" that they have little time or energy for supervising homework.

An increased responsibility is therefore placed upon teachers. As one teacher explained, "I see some of these mothers look very relieved when they drop off their kids in the morning. It's as if they are passing me the buck and glad about it." Even in homes where both parents are present, the demands of modern life— working, cooking, cleaning, just resting, and so on—tend to pull parents away from homework supervision and general encouragement regarding school. Teachers have picked up extra responsibilities from all sorts of families.

Many wonderful teachers are overworked. Many have had their spirits broken. What a sad state of affairs! We expect a lot from our schoolteachers, including the role of making up for increasingly absent or overworked parents. And while we expect so much, we value teachers very little. One of the most obvious indications of this is that teachers are poorly paid. Many other professions are higher on the socioeconomic ladder.

The sad but undeniable truth is that when we value our children's teachers so very little, we also are valuing our children very little. What are we saying about our own value systems by downgrading schoolteaching as a profession? Teaching is some of the most important work ever done.

When we complain about our schools and teachers, it is important to remember that we created them. Public or private, we pay into their budgets via taxes and tuitions. If we do not like what we see, then it is our responsibility to do more than complain. We must help; we must get involved.

Chapter 5

Evaluating Your Choice
of Preschools
and Schools

the LiTT Le wiat
hors

wons apon a tim
tor WUS a hors
the hors was
sad But it soon
FUWND a Frend
the END

Once you have taken human form, you will never be able
to live with your family under the waves again.
                    —The Sea Witch to the Little Mermaid in
                    Hans Christian Andersen's *The Little Mermaid*

Schools have a profound effect on children's mental development.
Good preschool and school experiences, such as academic success, approval from teachers, and positive recognition by peers,
can help children realize their mental potentials. Bad experiences,
such as academic failure, discipline problems, and embarrassment
in front of peers, can have the opposite effect, stifling children's
minds, suppressing the realization of their mental potentials, and
shattering their self-esteem.

   Choosing a school for a child is therefore a great responsibility. But parents do not always have a choice when it comes to the
schools, preschools, and day-care programs their children attend.
As I have explained elsewhere, the three controlling basics, *cost*,
convenience, and *choice*, are always at work. [1] If parents cannot
afford to pay the tuition at a particular school or program, their
children are not likely to attend it. (This is the basic problem of
cost.) Even when parents can afford to choose between several
educational programs because the programs are either part of the
public school system, or publicly subsidized, or employer spon-
sored, or church supported, or simply because the parents have
enough money to choose freely, convenience is a powerful limita-
tion. When the desired program is too far away, when it requires
a long commute through congested traffic, when it requires travel
in the direction opposite the parents' commute to work, or when
the hours just do not fit their schedules, parents may find it too
inconvenient to enroll their children. (This is the basic problem

of convenience.) Above all, even if cost and convenience are not issues, choice is a profoundly limiting factor. All too often, parents find that the type of school or preschool experience they want for their children is either entirely unavailable or so limited that there are long waiting lists and competitive admissions processes. The demand for quality education appears to exceed the supply. (This is the basic problem of choice.) So it is that the problems of cost, convenience, and choice dictate to a large degree the quality of a child's educational experience.

These overarching limitations of cost, convenience, and choice on parents' selections of schools for their children are so very powerful that, in fact, there really is no selection involved for most parents most of the time. They simply have to take what they can get for their children. I nevertheless offer, on the following pages, a few special notes on the selection of schools and preschools.

This chapter gives more attention to the selection of pre-school and day-care programs than it does to K–12 schools. This is because, at present, in the absence of a large public preschool system, and with so many mothers of young children in the labor force, more parents are feeling pressured to try to be selective at the preschool level. Once kindergarten begins, the majority of parents either prefer to or must rely on their local public schools to educate their children. Since most public school districts do not yet offer parents much choice in the way of schools or teachers, as a group, parents of what we call school-age children are exercising far less choice than those of preschool-age children. The result is that there is a great deal of dissatisfaction and frustration among parents. A certain amount of surrender to prevailing conditions takes place and, in the end, the children pay.

SELECTING AND EVALUATING PRESCHOOLS

If you are the parent of a preschool child, you should be well informed about the effects of preschool and the characteristics of various preschools before you make your decision about pre-school. Getting well informed can be a problem. There is disagreement among the experts in the field of early childhood education.

Take the debate about academic preschool. On the one hand, long-term gains in academic achievement do not appear great enough to justify parents' financial investments in intensively academic early childhood education. On the other hand, early learning is definitely possible and many children are not presented with enough academic stimulation and structure in their early years. Early childhood education may allow a child to enter kindergarten and first grade with experience, independence, and confidence. It may also lead to competence in basic reading, spelling, and math. However, the effects of academic pressure on preschool children may be psychologically damaging. Intensive early childhood education may benefit young children by teaching them to learn and to respond to structure rather than by teaching them specific skills. Yet highly structured and regimented early childhood education may put too much pressure on young children. It places great emphasis on achievement and measurable progress at a very young age. Moreover, because young children do not have much self-discipline, the discipline that may be applied and expected in intensive early childhood educational programs may be too extreme. Young children can be damaged by stress just as can adults.

In the face of this sort of debate, there can be no single correct answer for all children. As a parent, you must make your decision about early childhood education personal. Ask yourself:

- Am I setting standards for my child that are unrealistically high or low?
- Whose standards are they? Mine or other people's?
- If I want my child to be an early achiever, a "superbaby," do I want this because that is what my friends want for their children? Or because that is what I want for my child?

- If I want my child to be an early achiever, a superbaby, do I want this because this is what I was or wish I had been?
- If I want to encourage my baby to be a superbaby, is there only one way and only one type of super that my baby can be?
- What choice will make my child happiest in the present?

Your decision regarding preschool should never be final. Monitor your child's well-being at and interest in preschool on a regular basis. Overall, schools are finding that children with some preschool experience adapt to kindergarten and first grade better than children who "leave home" for the first time at age 5. However, some research is suggesting that children who enter full-time, out-of-home day care by age 1 and remain in such care until kindergarten may have discipline, concentration, and other learning problems in elementary school. Pay close attention to the effects of preschool or day care on your child.

Many parents consciously choose to de-emphasize the educational aspects of preschool and, instead, turn to nonacademic preschool or day-care programs. In the interviews I have conducted with hundreds of parents of young children, I have heard parents saying again and again, "I want my child to feel secure and loved most of all," "I need to know that someone will comfort my child when she cries," "I want him to have fun when I'm not around," "I don't want her to be too regimented and then hate the place." Day-care and preschool choices are matters of personal preference. Being clear on what your preferences are will help you choose a program. You may not find a program that satisfies all of your preferences, but you will at least have some criteria for making a choice.

List all of your personal preferences in the day-care/preschool arena and organize them in order of their importance to you. Some preference areas I recommend that you include are:

- *Love and affection.* Are you looking for a place that emphasizes one-to-one love and affection between staff members and your child to encourage the child's sense of security away from home? Or do you prefer a program with a more social emphasis, where children learn to feel at home in a group? Maybe you prefer a mix of these approaches.

- *Educational approach.* Do you want formal education or informal education for your child? If you prefer formal education, consider what subjects are important to you, for example, reading, mathematics, music, foreign languages, and art. If you prefer a less formal learning program, what kinds of activities would you like to see your child involved in? At what age do you want your child to begin these activities?

- *Religious orientation.* Religion or no religion? If you seek religion for your child, do you prefer a particular one?

- *Child preference.* Which program does your child prefer? This difficult question is one that you must continue to ask yourself and your child as your child grows.

Other areas of personal preference that are important include: discipline, food, nap time and its length, the age range of children at the school, the ethnic composition of the group, the ages of the staff, the qualifications of staff, the location of the day-care program and, of course, its cost.

Selecting a preschool or day-care program also requires careful attention to safety and protection matters. Some of these are:

- *Safety of the grounds.* Can the children get into the street? Are there places where they can fall? Is the building ventilated? Are there an adequate number of exits?

- *Safety of the equipment and the toys.* Is the playground equipment in good repair? Is it sharp and rusty? Are the toys safe for children your child's age?

- *Staff–child ratio.* Are there enough adults to pay attention to each child's safety?

- *Cleanliness and hygiene.* Are the bathrooms clean? Are the tables and chairs clean? Is the place regularly cleaned? Do the staff members wash their hands often and thoroughly and ask the children to do the same? What are the rules about sick children? Are sick children separated from the well children? Are they sent home? What would you like to have happen?

- *Licensing.* Does the program operate under a state or municipal license? If it does not, why not? Licenses guarantee at least some degree of quality, especially regarding staff–child ratios, square footage per child, safety standards, and the general and educational qualifications of the caretakers or teachers.

The decisions parents make about their preschool-age children are some of the most important decisions they will ever make. The preschool experience can mold a child's later adjustment to elementary school. Always pay attention to your heart and your mind when you visit a preschool or day-care program. The well-being of today's preschoolers affects the well-being of tomorrow's world.

I have included in this chapter a checklist for parents who seek guidance in making these important choices. This checklist is excerpted from my book *The Day Care Dilemma.* [2] You can modify this list to fit your personal opinions about what makes preschool and day care good by adding, taking out, or changing questions. Ask the questions that best express what you are looking for in a day-care or preschool program.

Use your list of questions as a score sheet. Make several copies of it and then fill one copy out for each preschool or day-care program that you are considering. Total each score sheet so that you have a rating for each day-care program. If you have asked yourself the appropriate questions, the program with the highest score will be the best for you.

Answer each question by circling a number from 1 through 5. A 5 is the highest score you can give. It means that you feel very good about a school or program in the category that the question asks about. A 3 is an in-between, neutral score. A 1 is the lowest score you can give. It means that you do not feel good about a school or program in the category the question asks about. Questions are not listed in order of importance.

Name of the program you are scoring _____

	Do not feel good about it		Feel neutral about it		Do feel good about it
	$1 \rightarrow$	$2 \rightarrow$	$3 \rightarrow$	$4 \rightarrow$	5

How do you feel about:

(1) The cleanliness of the place where this program operates?	1	2	3	4	5
(2) The safety of the environment?	1	2	3	4	5
(3) The safety of the neighborhood?	1	2	3	4	5
(4) The quality of the toys?	1	2	3	4	5
(5) The amount of space available per child?	1	2	3	4	5
(6) The meals and snacks fed to the children?	1	2	3	4	5
(7) The general health of the children enrolled in this program?	1	2	3	4	5
(8) The general health of the staff who work in this program?	1	2	3	4	5
(9) The time spent on physical activities?	1	2	3	4	5

(*continued*)

		Do not feel good about it		Feel neutral about it		Do feel good about it
		$1 \rightarrow$	$2 \rightarrow$	$3 \rightarrow$	$4 \rightarrow$	5
(10)	The balance of males to females among staff?	1	2	3	4	5
(11)	The balance of males to females among children?	1	2	3	4	5
(12)	The age range of the staff?	1	2	3	4	5
(13)	The age range of the children?	1	2	3	4	5
(14)	The way the rules are enforced?	1	2	3	4	5
(15)	The opportunities for family involvement?	1	2	3	4	5
(16)	The overall educational philosophy?	1	2	3	4	5
(17)	The types of educational activities?	1	2	3	4	5
(18)	The amount of time spent on prereading skills?	1	2	3	4	5
(19)	How well prepared the staff are to teach children?	1	2	3	4	5
(20)	The amount of quiet time?	1	2	3	4	5
(21)	The amount of nap time?	1	2	3	4	5
(22)	The amount of one-to-one attention children get from staff?	1	2	3	4	5
(23)	The amount of affection children get from staff?	1	2	3	4	5
(24)	The distance of this day-care program from your home?	1	2	3	4	5
(25)	The distance of this day-care program from your workplace?	1	2	3	4	5

(*continued*)

	Do not feel good about it		Feel neutral about it		Do feel good about it
	$1 \rightarrow$	$2 \rightarrow$	$3 \rightarrow$	$4 \rightarrow$	5
(26) The hours this program is open?	1	2	3	4	5
(27) The salaries of the staff?	1	2	3	4	5
(28) The cost of this care?	1	2	3	4	5
(29) The overall quality of this day-care program?	1	2	3	4	5

Total score for this day-care or preschool program _____

Again, there are many items other than those on the above checklist to consider. Remember to check the program for a current license and liability insurance. Check the history of the program: How long has it been there? How much turnover has there been among children and staff? If the program rents or leases space, what is the duration of the rental agreement or lease? Could it shut down on you when you need it most and after your children have become attached to it?

There is a lot about preschool and child care that is difficult to assign a score to. I once visited a program that received rave reviews from parents and top professionals. I myself was quite impressed and scored the program highly on my rating scale. But the next day, when I drove by, I saw one of the child-care workers from the program walking down the street with nine children from the program. She had no other adults with her. The children were not holding hands and they were stepping in and out of the street. The traffic was very heavy and the children were clearly out of her control. Yes, a high-scoring program was failing in the very basic area of safety.

Many parents of preschool-age children are now weighing

the financial and career rewards gained when both parents work away from home against the loss of irreplaceable contact with and closer supervision of their children. There is no right or wrong way or easy solution for any of us. This is one of life's choices that each family must make. And, as I noted earlier, all too often there is no choice. Economic necessity and long child-care program waiting lists leave parents with few real options. They feel forced to place their child in any affordable and available program.

CHILD ABUSE IN DAY-CARE AND EDUCATIONAL SETTINGS

Even when parents have no choice as to what program or school their children attend, parents do have a choice as to whether or not they monitor its quality. I have listed many elements of quality above. Because so many parents are concerned about child neglect and abuse in out-of-home care and school settings, and because neglect and abuse can have serious negative effects on a child's self-esteem and ongoing mental development, I include the following discussion. This is of special concern for parents of children who may be too young to report to their parents or to know when they are being neglected or abused.

Before beginning this discussion, I must remind my readers that the rate of child abuse in day care, preschool, and school is very low when compared to the rate of child abuse occurring in children's own homes. Some people may claim that this is because child abuse in day care is more underreported than child abuse in the home. However, abuse is more likely to take place behind closed doors. Child day-care and preschool settings are generally more public than private homes. Parents pick up their children at various hours of the day and sometimes drop in unannounced.

If your child-care, preschool, or school program does not

allow unscheduled or even scheduled visits from parents, you would do well to inquire immediately as to why. Parents have a right to know what goes on there. Parents have a right to visit. Certainly, parents dropping in unannounced at any hour of the day can be disruptive. So do not view a scheduling requirement as a sign of problems. But make certain that you visit—more than once. And do drop in a few times during the course of the year.

Another note. Children go through many different phases of personality development. Some blatant changes in a child's temperament, including fear and mood swings, are to be expected as a child grows and experiences new aspects of the world. Sudden expressions of dissatisfaction with day care or school may simply be normal developmental expressions. However, parents would do well to remain alert to such changes because they may be indications of problems.

Be very careful when you suspect abuse. Abuse is only one of the possible problems a child may be expressing when he or she is upset about going to school, be it preschool or day care (or elementary school for that matter). Maybe other stressful changes have occurred. Aggression between children? A person on the staff? New children in the class? A favorite friend gone? A new room? Increased competition for toys, books, or attention?

And what about the child's life at home? Has anything happened in your home life in recent months? Family breakup? Money worries? Unemployment? A move to a new neighborhood? New fights with a sibling? Birth of a new child? Drug or alcohol problems? Other stresses? These things are felt by children as well as adults. It is quite possible that a child may express feelings about family problems by projecting them onto the day-care or school situation. And, without realizing it, many parents would rather think that day care is the source of the child's anxiety than to feel that family life has caused the child's upset.

Many working parents feel some degree of guilt about leaving their young children in the care of nonfamily members for all or a portion of the day several days a week. Quite often, parents are not fully in touch with the guilt that they feel. But somewhere deep inside, there is a gnawing in the stomach, a vague sense of insecurity, an irrational fear. Parents have the often unspoken sense that they are neglecting and perhaps even abusing or abandoning their children by dropping them off and leaving them in the care of someone whom they do not know extremely well. In most cases, parental guilt about preschool and day care is most apparent when parents first enroll their children in the program. Soon both parents and children grow accustomed to the arrangement. Many children grow to love the program staff and the peer contact they receive there. This sometimes leaves parents with unacknowledged and deeply buried feelings of guilt and resentment about leaving their children. By elementary school, most parents are over this guilt, but they may still feel uncomfortable about their choice—or lack of choice—of school for their children.

Most of the child-care, preschool, and teaching staff I have met are wonderful, giving people. Get to know the people who work with and teach your child. How do you feel about them? How does your child relate to them? Take the time to get your questions answered. Examine closely your reactions to your child's teachers or caregivers and your own guilt regarding placing your child in their care at what may seem a young age to you. If you are left with concerns about child abuse, then the situation warrants more of your attention. Pay attention to this, if for no other reason than that you need to put yourself at ease.

Having said all this, I must again say that some instances of child abuse and neglect do occur in day-care, preschool, and school settings and that this can be extremely damaging to its victims as well as to the other children who see it happening. Just seeing my school principal beat a boy who was misbehaving in my third-grade class ruined the rest of the school year for me—and I was not the one being punished. Child abuse is one of the most despicable crimes imaginable. It is important for all of us, whether parents or not, to be on the lookout for the signs of child abuse.

Let us focus first on physical abuse. Physical abuse is relatively easy to spot. If a child has bruises, welts, lacerations, burns, and broken bones that seem to go far beyond what he or she would receive in normal child's play, be alerted to the fact that the child is enduring some kind of extreme physical aggression. Extremely disturbing experiences such as physical violence usually result in behavioral indications such as (1) reversion to bedwetting in children who have quit wetting the bed (usually seen in children under 7 years of age); (2) wincing or jerking away when adults approach or reach to touch them; (3) extreme fear of a person or place; (4) extremes in behavior; and (5) unexplainable mood swings including listlessness, detachment, and aggression.

Indications of sexual abuse may include the above and also more specific signs. If a child has been sexually abused, you may see that the child has difficulty in walking or sitting, experiences pain when urinating, or has pain, swelling, itching, bleeding, or discharge in the genital area. Signs of venereal disease are, of course, an indication that sexual abuse has occurred. (And certainly, the possible threat of HIV infection haunts any parent who has to deal with these issues. A test for such infection may be suggested by the child's doctor.)

Children who have been or are being sexually abused tend to exhibit some of the changes in behavior that children who have experienced physical violence exhibit. In addition to these changes, in sexually abused children you may also find sudden changes in sleeping or eating habits, poor peer relations, poor self-image, abrupt changes in school performance, compulsive masturbation, excessive nightmares about which the child cannot be consoled, and bizarre, sophisticated, or sexual behavior beyond the child's years. Remember, all of these symptoms may be symptoms of abuse. But they can also be symptoms of other stressful events in a child's life.

Children usually let us know that they are going through something unpleasant when indeed they are. Alas, parents do not always know how to read or recognize the signs. We have to learn to hear or see what our children are telling us. Sometimes, other children will report that a child is being or has been abused. And sometimes, a child will reveal that he or she is being abused by telling part of the story or by saying that there is something he or she cannot tell. Listen to your child. And listen to yourself. You may already know what you need to know. If you suspect child abuse, call your local child abuse council or county social services and get directions about how to report and what to do for help. You can also call local and national child abuse hotlines.

Whether the problem that your child is experiencing is the result of abuse or of something else, if you continue to feel concerned about abuse and neglect, seek a professional assessment of your child's condition. If at any time you are worried about your child's adjustment to school or preschool, follow up on this concern by talking to the child, other children, the teacher, other teachers, and other parents. If your concerns are not dispelled, then do take your child to professionals such as social workers, psychologists, and medical doctors.

HARASSMENT AND OTHER ABUSE
OF OLDER CHILDREN

Child abuse and neglect does not magically end at a certain age. We do, however, expect older children to fend off offensive gestures and assaults and to report problems to adults. Our expectations are warranted; older children do take care of themselves in ways the young ones do not. However, all too often, cases of harassment and other infringements upon the rights and well-being of our adolescents are discovered too late. For example, there is an emerging awareness of the problem of sexual harassment in the junior high and high schools, in which subtle (and sometimes overt) innuendos, gestures, and approaches are made from teacher to student, from staff to student, from older student to younger student, and sometimes even from student to teacher. Open dialogues with young people about these possibilities and how to report them are necessary. At the same time, it is essential that we be on the lookout for false accusations directed at teachers who, for some reason, have been selected for attack by students with problems.

While the entire matter of sexual harassment in the schools warrants at least book-length attention, I will say but a few more words on the issue here. There is another much more common problem than inappropriate sexual advances and innuendos being directed at students from older students and teachers. There is a subtle and continuing undercurrent of sexual bias regarding the differences in academic capabilities of boys and girls at various ages and the differences in the training they require. Some of these biases are overcompensated for and thus reversed—as when we find parents and teachers encouraging girls more strongly than boys. Others of these biases are so very deeply buried that they go almost entirely undetected. It is no longer commonly the case to hear a high-school calculus teacher tell the two or three girls in his class, "I don't give girls A's" (as I was told), but the attitudes may still be present in some adults. Students feel the unspoken attitudes of their parents and teachers. We must make it possible to discuss these whenever it may be necessary.

SELECTING AND EVALUATING SCHOOLS

If you are in a position to be choosing an elementary, junior high, or high school for your child, you are fortunate. Many parents have no choice regarding the K–12 education of their children. In choosing a school, consider some of the basics listed below. You will find that the basics you emphasize reflect your personal taste, your child's age, your child's preferences, and the preferences of your child's friends, as well as the auspice under which the school functions—public or private, church or unaffiliated, profit or nonprofit.

The atmosphere. What is your and your child's reaction to:

- The relative mix of racial and ethnic characteristics among both the students and the teachers.
- The mechanisms available for answering parents' questions and concerns and for hearing students' or their parents' complaints.
- The degree of cooperation among teachers and staff.
- The involvement of parents and family members.
- The school's responsiveness to individual needs and religions and its respect for individual temperaments.
- The sense of community.
- The official philosophy of the school, if it has one.

The structure. What is your and your child's reaction to:

- The attention to discipline, limits, and rules.
- The amount of structured learning time built into the daily program.
- The use of psychological screening, admissions, and general academic tests.

The psychology. What is your and your child's reaction to:

- The amount of personal involvement on the part of teachers in their teaching activities, including the amount of one-to-one, personal attention delivered with appropriate affection, warmth, and physical contact.
- The extent to which teachers effectively manage psychological upsets and traumas.
- The degree to which transition times (arrivals and departures of students) are smoothly planned and executed.

The education. What is your and your child's reaction to:

- The clarity of educational philosophy and program design.
- The effects of any preenrollment screening for mental or educational level (the procuring of treatment for those identified as learning-disabled individuals and the use of special classes for the gifted or those with special needs or interests).
- The degree of sensory and mental stimulation.
- The extent of academic instruction.
- The opportunities for creative and civic expression.
- The training in practical skills.

There are no right or wrong responses to the above list of school characteristics. Everyone has his or her own preferences when it comes to schooling—much goes into the selection of a school. While curriculum is very important, a good curriculum in a terrible atmosphere is not going to provide a positive school experience. Conversely, a wonderful and loving school environment in the absence of good academic training is hardly a school.

When I evaluate a school, I want to know something about each of the items I listed above. I also take a very close look at the averages and ranges of the children's achievement test scores. While standardized test scores do not tell the whole story, they do determine the school placement and school admissions futures (admissions into high schools and colleges) of our children. If the school I am evaluating has a low achievement test average compared to the average on the same test at other schools, I know that the children graduating from the low-average school are having difficulty competing, at least on paper. Again, test scores are not everything. But test scores are powerful. They talk. They follow our children.

One thing I try to avoid in my evaluating of a school is looking at its overall student body grade averages. Parents tell me they ask schools about this quite often. Grade averages mean very little in terms of the quality of the school. A school can have an overall student body grade average of A−, but this does not necessarily mean that the school is doing a fantastic job of educating all of its students. It may mean that the school grades much too easily. It may mean that the school "inflates" the grade averages so that the school will look good and so that more of its students will be admitted to elite high schools and universities. I have seen this, especially at the high-school level, all too often. I have found many public and private high schools guilty in this area. And the students are the ones hurt by this. A child who should be getting C's and is, instead, getting B's or B+'s or even A−'s is being misinformed. I have seen college freshmen in tears, claiming, "I was an A student in chemistry in high school and now I'm a B− student, and I'm studying much harder now. Why is this happening to me?" In many cases, this is happening because the high school let its students believe that they were performing at higher levels, studying more and learning more than they actually were. While this may be a pleasant illusion for students while it is happening, they often pay in serious ways later.

Visit the classrooms of the schools you are evaluating. Watch what happens there. Do you like the vigor, the structure, the content, and the spirit of the teaching in *each* subject? Does your child?

Talk to the parents and students who are presently involved with the school. How do they answer the questions I have asked in this chapter? Most importantly, talk to as many graduates of the school and their parents as you can. They will tell you a lot that the school will not say—both positive and negative. Remember, you and your child are the consumers of education, you pay for it one way or another, and you have a right to be well-informed consumers.

Chapter 6

Easing the Transition
from Home to School

79

> Once I was a marionette, as I am now, but I did not like to study and I ran away from home. One day I was changed into a donkey . . .
>
> —Pinocchio
> to the poor man who bought the donkey
> in C. Colladi's *Pinocchio: The Story of a Marionette*

The explicit purpose of school is to educate, to educate in cognitive, physical, and social areas. Home is less formal and neither explicitly nor exclusively focused on education. School and home are thus substantially different. No matter how relaxed and undirected a classroom may be, it is most definitely a *formal learning environment*. The learning environment of school has the effect of formalizing learning through the use of lesson plans, the giving of assignments, the grading of work, the specification of academic levels, and other efforts that serve to structure the learning process.

THE CHILD IN THE
FORMAL LEARNING ENVIRONMENT

When a child begins to attend school, learning becomes connected with the school setting. Although learning occurs in all settings, not just in school, most nonschool learning occurs so informally that it takes place unbeknownst to the learner. What is it that actually happens when learning is moved from home to school, when learning is therefore formalized? Unlike home, in the school setting, students are told, "Today (or this week, this month, this semester) we will learn about earthworms." In this way, the expectation of learning about something in particular is established. This expectation of learning is a two-way street. The student expects to be taught about the stated subject (earthworms, in this case) and the teacher expects the student to learn what he or she teaches. As children move up the grade levels, they are held increasingly accountable for the content of lessons and courses, usually via assignments and tests.

Even in the early (K–2) years of elementary school, children feel the presence of these formal expectations. In the beginning, in preschool and kindergarten, school expectations are felt in social more than academic areas. Children are expected to take turns, stay in line, sit still at circle time, restrict "bathroom talk" to the bathroom, and so on. In this way, they are eased into or acculturated to the school environment. School expectations build slowly, over time, through the years. Still, these formal school expectations, whether they are academic or social, create a sense of pressure.

HELPING CHILDREN EXCEL
AT FORMAL LEARNING

In the right form and dose, pressure is positive. It contributes to development. Some children respond to the pressure of the formal expectations of school with excellent work. They enjoy the challenge of expectation. They seek the approval, the status, the attention, and the self-esteem that come from doing well. Good grades feel good.

Clearly stated expectations in the form of assignments tend to be more frequently found at school than at home. These expectations require clearly defined responses from the children. "Draw a picture of this insect on this paper, using the brown felt pen" is a clearly stated expectation, the sort that is more commonly heard at school than at home. By contrast, the question, "Why don't you go and do something quiet for a while?" is not a clearly stated expectation but a vaguely stated question that is more typically heard at home than at school. Parents are not trained in the art of giving their children clear assignments nor are they expected to have had such training.

Most children appreciate the clarity of formal and explicit commands such as the one above ("Draw a picture . . ."). This is because they understand precisely what they should do, and they know that they are really expected to do it. The expectation is clear. There is no doubt in the child's mind about the requirement.

Even if stated as an expectation rather than a question, the unclear command, "Go do something quiet for a while," while allowing freedom of choice, leaves much room for failure to meet the expectation. The command is so vague that it raises a question about the need to comply. And the command leaves doubt regarding the path to approval. If one should comply, how would compliance look? After all, a child might go do something "quiet for a while," such as paint the furniture green or put a towel in the toilet, and receive no approval at all. How does a child meet such a poorly formulated expectation?

A child who feels confident about his or her ability to satisfy formal expectations and who enjoys a sense of success when he or she does satisfy expectations can excel at formal learning. Parents can give their children a head start on school success by making their expectations at least as clear and honest as those their children will find in school. Below, I provide some guidelines for clear expectations.

- Practice stating clearly and specifically what you want your child to do.
- Make certain that your demands and expectations can be met. For example, do not expect a child in kindergarten to do advanced calculus. You can teach this and believe that this is possible (I do), but do not make demands unless you are absolutely certain that they can be met.

- Be sure that you really mean it when you state an expectation.
- When your child meets the clearly stated expectation, give the child approval. Let the child know that he or she has met the specific expectation.
- If the child has tried, but has not entirely met your expectations, do not emphasize what has been done correctly and incorrectly. Focus instead on the fact that a genuine effort has been made to meet the expectation.

Some children are overwhelmed by the formal expectations made of them in the school environment. Sometimes assignments may seem too difficult, too big, too unfamiliar. But much of the time, these children simply *lack experience* in completing challenging (and even simple) assignments. If your child is, or may occasionally be, one of these children, you can help your child discover that he or she *is* able to satisfy formal expectations. Using the above list, you can help your child practice at home. All children, regardless of their personalities, benefit from parents' efforts to communicate their expectations clearly. Begin as early in the child's life as possible. And, if you have not started early, it is never too late.

EASING THE TRANSITION

We cannot, except perhaps by remembering our own first school experiences, know how strikingly different the home environment is from the school environment. You may, on the one hand, recall your first week in kindergarten. Maybe you remember noticing that your mother did not come running when you cried, that your bed was not there, that you could not eat anytime you wanted to, that you received less attention, or on a more positive note, that there were more children to play with and more group activities in which to engage. On the other hand, you may recall nothing of this first week of school.

Even if a child is happy, proud, and thrilled to start school, a shock of some sort is experienced. By all outer appearances, most children overcome this shock and adapt, in an hour, a day, or a month. Yet the shock does not go away. Instead, it is internalized. It is buried so deeply in our children that parents often fail to continue to help ease the transition from home to school. This help is needed long after outer signs of shock disappear. It is needed even when no signs of shock appear at the outset. The critical transition from home to school continues through every day of the child's school year and school life.

So let us focus now on methods of easing the transition from home to school. The methods I list below apply to:

- the first entry into school (day care, nursery school, or preschool) in early childhood.
- the reentry at the start of every school year (from preschool through twelfth grade).
- the event of moving to a new school or a new class within the same school.
- the transitions back into the school setting at the end of summer, winter, and spring vacations.

School psychologists tell me that these methods should also apply to returns to school following doctors appointments, absences, and weekends. Above all, these methods of easing transition are an important part of the success of *each* school day:

- Always officially recognize the beginning of a school year, semester, week, and day. Do the same for returns to school after holidays and after absences. Do not leave the child to experience the transition and any feelings associated with it on his or her own. This is how the "I don't wanna go back to school" attitude begins and ends up being repeated regularly. The child feels something about going back to school, cannot quite label it or describe its complexity, and grabs the most ready description of it. So help the child by labeling all the back-to-school transitions. Say regularly, "Tomorrow (or today) you go back to school."

• Establish little rituals that mark these transitions and then stick to them. For example, Sunday night marks the end of the weekend and the beginning of the school week. Say so: "It is Sunday evening. Tomorrow is Monday, the first day of the school week. So we will do what we regularly do to get ready for the school week," or "to end our weekend." Adopt and stick to regular Sunday night rituals. These might include:

> a long bath and hair washing
> a family circle or family reading time
> an organization of the child's schedule for the coming week
> a phone call to grandparents
> a review of all homework or subjects being studied

• Put together a list of your Sunday back-to-school activities. Post it somewhere where the child can see it easily, even if the child does not yet read. Also establish school-night rituals. These can include:

> laying out of the next day's clothes
> packing the school bag
> making the lunch if one is required

• For big transitions, such as those following a midyear or summer vacation, use a wall calendar posted where your child can see it. Mark the days off in one color and put a star or pleasant-colored box around each first day of school after a vacation. The first day of a new school year should have its own special color of mark. If the child is old enough, have the child mark the calendar.

RESPECTING CHILDREN'S DIFFERENCES

Remember that while children are quite predictable, every one of them has his or her own idiosyncrasies. Children are different. They react to school differently at different times of the year, at different ages, in different family circumstances. Each child's special reaction evolves over time.

So many things affect a child's reaction to school. A parent cannot shelter a child from everything that might generate a minor but negative reaction to school. Such sheltering, or attempts at such sheltering, infantilizes a child, keeping him or her dependent on the parent long past the natural age of such dependency. Instead, a parent must be as aware as possible of all influences on the particular child and the gravity of them. Labeling these influences for the child and discussing them in a way that does not predict a negative effect is important. Tell the child that you think a disagreement with friends (or whatever you think it is) could be bothering him or her. Ask if you are on the right track. Encourage the child to label his or her own difficulties. Discuss ways that the child might handle problems on his or her own.

THE HOME LIFE BEHIND SCHOOL STRESS

School can be a stressful experience for a child. However, before parents and teachers seek to tackle the sources of school stress, it is essential that they examine the home life of the child. When a child resists going to school, performs or behaves poorly at school, or has difficulty paying attention in class, the child may be bringing problematic elements of his or her home life to school.

1. Examine the amount of sleep the child gets. This is true for children of all ages. Examine your child's sleeping environment.

Where is his or her bedroom in relation to the nearest street with vehicular traffic? Can you move this bedroom to a quieter part of your house or apartment? Consider placing heavier curtains or some sort of heavy material over the windows at night. Is this bedroom near a noisy, vibrating refrigerator? If so, it can be turned down at night or you can put an automatic timer on it.

2.   *Examine the way your child organizes his or her time.* Does he or she go to sleep early enough to wake up without an alarm? Look beyond the amount of sleep to your child's general use of time. Is he or she often rushed in the morning? Does he or she have time for a satisfying breakfast? Plan your child's day so that that child can get what he or she needs while doing what must be done. No last-minute rushing. It *is* possible to do this. Organize your child's time so that he or she spends it instead of it spending the child. Place a daily schedule on the wall.

3.   *Examine your child's eating habits.* Does your child have at least a piece of fruit or some juice to break the nightlong fast in the morning? I say "at least" here because some children are not hungry very early in the morning. Pressuring these children to eat a hearty breakfast before school starts the day with psychological and, often, gastric distress. And do not give your child empty-calorie, nonnutritious, sugary foods, caffeine, or coffee before school. You would not be able to drive your car very far on bad fuel or on empty. Treat your child's body at least as well as you treat your vehicle. Whatever the time of day, cut out junk fuels such as caffeine and white sugar and give your child's body some real food. (Remember, sugar-covered jelly doughnuts do not qualify as quality fuel.) Note also that proteins such as those in eggs, cheeses, and meat may be too heavy for some children to consume in the morning. Try complex carbohydrates, such as those found in whole-grain breads and cereals, for breakfast and provide proteins later in the day.

4.   *Examine your child's level of physical exercise.* Teach your child to stretch a few minutes at the beginning and at the end of

each day. Stretching stimulates blood flow and reduces stress. Watch your child to see if he or she tends to be lazy and inactive. Talk to your child's teacher for another perspective on your child's level of physical activity. While many children are naturally physically active, some are not. Emotional problems, lack of sleep, improper nutrition, and even the television addiction described in Chapter 7 can lead to decreased physical activity in a child. If this is so for your child, then build in physical activity such as dance, sports, or gymnastics classes. If your child is shy, or if you cannot provide such classes, get out and play games like tag and basketball with your child. These are great fun and you can probably use the exercise yourself.

5. *Examine your child's home life and social life.* Does home feel like a safe place to go? Does your child have the opportunity to make deep and satisfying contact with all family members? How about friends? Does your child have ample opportunity to play with friends of the same age? Does your child have a close friend, someone to share secrets with? These are essential in a child's life.

6. *If you live more than five minutes from school, examine your child's commuting activities.* If you drive, try to use your commute time in a healthy way. The trips you and your child make to and from school are expenditures of valuable time. These minutes add up to hours and weeks. And the weeks turn into years. This is the time of your child's life (as well as of your own), so use it well. Find audio tapes that are fun or soothing to sing along with or listen to. Try singing together without tapes. Talk about fun or interesting topics. Be available if your child wants to talk about a personal problem; however, do not introduce painful topics or disciplinary actions on the way to or from school. Do not force conversation during these trips; volunteer it and respond to what your child says.

7. *Look for other possible areas of stress outside of school.* Make a game out of it. Be a detective. Investigate everything thoroughly. Remember that there are many sources of, kinds of, and reactions

to stress. Be very aware. Come face-to-face with the sources of your child's stress. You may find that your stress or that of your spouse is a primary source. Many of your own stressors can be changed, just as can your child's. Many of your own stressors can be made to seem less stressful and more manageable when you simply begin eating, sleeping, and exercising regularly. Stressful lifestyles can be reorganized. As you reorganize your child's life, reorganize your own. You must commit to this reorganization of yourself as well as of your child for you and your child to feel the benefits. See a counselor or psychotherapist if you cannot manage your stress on your own.

CHILDHOOD HYPOCHONDRIA

All too often, children feign illness to miss a day of school. Strangely enough, this happens even when home life is more stressful than school life. Because of its significance, let us focus for a moment on some critical aspects of childhood hypochondria.

The need for attention and care. A child exhibiting symptoms of physical illness may get more attention for his or her physical pain than he or she would get for emotional pain. When a deep need (and sometimes a merely mild need) for attention and care is not being met, hypochondria may feel like the next best way to get what is desperately wanted.

The fostering of dependence by family members. Family members can inadvertently encourage hypochondriacal symptoms in a child by placing emphasis on physical problems above all other forms of expression and by responding more to physical illness than to other "less tangible" experiences of family members.

The need to manipulate others. Feeling powerless in a family or social setting can lead some children to resort to physical symptoms. These symptoms can serve as a way to make requests and even demands upon parents and other caregivers for time and attention that they would not otherwise give.

The desire for whatever advantages the "sick role" brings. Having discovered that the sick role brings control over others and draws attention, some children use this behavior again and again.

A way to avoid the demands of life. We all have at least contemplated staying home from school or even from work to avoid demands. This is a natural inclination. However, unchecked hypochondria can become a way of staying home from life to avoid its demands and responsibility. Work with this problem while your child is young. Be sensitive to your child's fears of what is out there in the world. Initiate, but do not force, discussions about fear and give your child the opportunity to hear you explain that everyone is afraid from time to time.

A response to difficulties of self-expression. When it is hard for a child to say what he or she is thinking or feeling, when a child has not learned outlets for emotions, the child may find an outlet for emotion by experiencing hypochondriacal symptoms.

A behavior learned from parents or relatives. Hypochondriacal behavior can run in families. Children tend to take on the behavioral styles of their parents or other relatives and then, later, pass these on to their own children. Examine your own and other family members' behaviors to see if you or someone else is setting this type of example for your child.

Intensely experienced events. These may also contribute to the development of childhood (and adulthood) hypochondria. Grieving the death of a loved one or witnessing a death (even on television) can bring with it physical pain and even symptoms similar to those experienced by the person who died.

The experience of a "real" physical illness. Children, especially during the preschool and early school years, tend to be preoccupied with their bodies. Illnesses and injuries can evoke strong responses and lasting memories, even when they are minor ones. These memories bring out hypochondria in some children, especially during or right after the actual recovery.

Whether or not it takes the form of hypochondria, the transition or expected transition back to or in and out of school on an annual, weekly, and even daily basis can create all kinds of anxiety. Without parents acknowledging this anxiety, a child is coping (or not coping) with that anxiety all alone. Establish a continuing dialogue with the child, one in which you both talk about mental and physical conditions and sensations. Do not tell your child what to feel. Do not tell your child that he or she does not feel sick if he or she claims to feel so. Listen and reflect on what you hear. The dialogue itself will relieve some of the child's tension.

Keep in mind that your child's mind and body are interconnected, as are your own. Mental biochemistry can create and regulate emotional pain. It can control physical pain. Emotional biochemistry can set physiological biochemistry into motion. Unpleasant feelings can cause sensations of sickness, just as sickness can cause unpleasant feelings. It works both ways. When your child has the flu, he or she can be grouchy, low in spirit. When your child is grouchy and low in spirit, he or she can develop nausea or a stomachache. The distinctions between mind and body are not cut and dry.

The transition from home to school is always felt to some degree. Although you cannot and should not solve all of your child's difficulties in life, you can be aware of the fact that children feel the transition. Just knowing that their parents understand this helps children.

Chapter 7

The Child in the Family Environment

At that moment, Cinderella's fairy godmother appeared, but only Cinderella could see her. With a wave of her magic wand, she turned Cinderella's rags into a gown even more beautiful than the one she had worn to the ball.

Her stepsisters then recognized Cinderella as the lovely princess from the ball. They knelt before her and apologized for treating her so badly. Then Cinderella, who was as kind as she was beautiful, said, "It's all right, sisters. I forgive you both."

—Samantha Easton,
Cinderella

Think of the family environment as the nest. This is the nurturing place in which the child's early survival is ensured. It is also the site in which the child's potential is stimulated or overlooked or thwarted as he or she ages. Parents seem to know this, almost instinctively, and are hungry for information about how to stimulate their children's minds from within the nest.

SUPERCHILD PRESSURE

"I want my child to be all that she can be." "I know my child can have a better career than I have." "Every generation of my family achieves more than the last." "I want my child to follow in her father's footsteps, not mine."

It is not surprising that parents want to know how to help their children become "superchildren," increasing their potentials to the limit. We see this in the superbaby preoccupation. However, the idea of superbabies comes from the same place as those superwomen and supermen ideas: the cabbage patch of the American dream as seen on television and in our imaginations. Wanting a child to be superintelligent and superaccomplished by kindergarten is a response to competitive pressure. It is also asking a child to do what many adults ask themselves to do: be a high achiever. Be invincible like a machine. The ideal machine is all-powerful, flawless, perfect, and, in a word, super. We dream that we and our children have the capacity to function like these ideal machines (the likes of which we have never seen in real life because machines break down).

This superbaby fascination is a modern luxury. Until the beginning of this century, physical survival was the primary objective of child-rearing. This is because over one in ten children died by the age of 5. For most parents, the question was not one of rearing a child but whether or not the child would survive to be reared at all. We are indeed fortunate to have a standard of living that allows us to dream of superbabies. When physical survival is at stake, intellectual training in early childhood is not an issue.

We have also changed our perceptions of childhood. Children were once viewed as property, additional helping hands and sources of income. Families depended on their children to help them survive. Now it is rare for a child to contribute to the family income until the late teens, if at all. Early childhood is now viewed as being the prime time in an individual's life. It is during this time that a human being's development can be most encouraged or most severely curtailed. In these early years of childhood, many modern parents, especially those of the white, upper middle class, see themselves as having the opportunity to produce and rear a superbaby: an individual who will grow into a superchild and into a person who will excel in adulthood. This superchild pressure puts children and their parents under a great deal of stress and must be avoided.

The payoff of this vision of the superchild is a super young person who has been trained to be successful in a society based on competitive individualism. Does the training pay off? Not necessarily. Do parents have to buy into it? No. What I suggest parents do instead is focus on their children's environments: Are they nurturing? Are they rich?

The rich family environment is nurturing. It ensures survival and goes beyond, stimulating development along many avenues. It is highly attentive to individual developmental needs. What this means is that, as a child grows and changes, the family environment responds to his or her changing needs.

THE SPECIAL ISSUE OF
GROWTH AND DEVELOPMENT

Because developmental changes are most dynamic, rapid, and crucial during early childhood, considerable research on growth and development has focused on children under age 6, or "preschool-age" children. The units of time allotted in the definition of developmental periods are shortest for the earliest years of life; these developmental units get larger as the child ages. This is seen in the following standard calendar of early childhood development:

Infancy (first year)
   Newborn (birth through 28 days)
   Early infancy (first through sixth month)
   Late infancy (seventh through twelfth month)
Toddlerhood (1 through 3 years of age)
   The "terrible twos" ($1\frac{1}{2}$ to $2\frac{1}{2}$ years)
   The "trusting threes" ($2\frac{1}{2}$ to $3\frac{1}{2}$ years)
Preschool age (4 up to or through 5 years of age) [1]

However helpful a chart like this one may seem, it does not say much about any one child's development. The ability to predict landmarks of normal growth and development is of limited use. Every individual develops at his or her own rate. Any time we fail to take into account a child's unique characteristics, we risk neglecting crucial responses to that child's needs. Familial care, that is, care provided by the family, along with care provided by friends and relatives, is less apt to overgeneralize from one child to the next than is care and education in a group or school setting. This is primarily because there are fewer children in the home and the caregivers, especially the parents, have a greater stake in the children's development. After all, they are related to the child. They have a *biological investment*. Hence, the care a child receives at home is usually the most important in that child's life.

Families can protect children from the overgeneralization that society imposes on them. Overgeneralization can have detrimental effects upon children. For example, a physically handicapped child of "normal" intelligence may be hindered in his or her development of academic competencies by environmental inadequacies, such as the lack of wheelchair access to the computer room at school. When skills deemed "normal" for that child's age cannot be developed, alternative skills and other behaviors emerge, sometimes precocious and other times more backward than expected. The danger is that essential steps in that child's development may occur but go unrecognized or, worse yet, may occur and be misinterpreted as deviant, when, all the while, the child is progressing normally for his or her special condition.

The comparison of any individual's development, whether he or she is considered to be "handicapped" or not, to a "normal" curve can lead to a serious misdiagnosis of intellectual ability. For a mildly retarded child, or one who is not retarded but fails to test well because of either physical disability, emotional problems, or bilingual difficulties, I.Q. and other types of academic tests can lead educators to the wrong conclusions. All too often, I have seen children of average and above-average intelligence labeled as retarded. The ensuing damage can be irreparable.

Other problematic applications of the notion of "normal" growth and development stem from a limited understanding of these concepts. The standard principles of growth and development, which are found in many hygiene and child development textbooks, are built upon the concepts of *growth*, which refers to any change in physical size; of *maturation*, which refers to the natural capacity of any individual to progress over time; of *learning*, which refers to the process of acquiring new skills and knowledge; and of *development*, which refers to any increase in competency due to maturation or learning. [2] Growth and development are thus the product of at least four processes that do not always occur together. Someone who is growing may not be learning. Someone who is growing older may be developing but will not be recognized as doing so because his or her changes are not interpreted as "growth." The effects of simple maturation or the passage of time may be interpreted as development when they are not. While parents and teachers must be very aware of children's growth, maturation, learning, and developmental curves, they must constantly strive not to misinterpret or overgeneralize them. A child may be behind other children of his own age in his ability to add fractions, but this does not necessarily mean he is developing too slowly. We all proceed at our own individual pace.

COMPONENTS OF
A RICH FAMILY ENVIRONMENT

The ideal family environment defends children against the overgeneralization and institutionalization they face in school and society.

Love and Other Emotional Contact

A child needs a place where feelings are openly and honestly acknowledged, where feelings are felt in a way a child can understand them. The family can be the first line of defense against what can seem to many a child to be a cold and impersonal world.

Let us assume that all children are wonderful beings. Each and every one of them is born with tremendous potential. No one knows for certain what guarantees the realization of that potential, but love is the best bet. Although love is a vague and difficult feeling to describe in terms of precise activities, it is important for parents to be certain that they:

- Communicate "I love you" regularly in words and in actions.
- Offer, but do not force, physical affection—hugs and kisses. These are great communicators of love. Do not go more than a day or two without offering physical affection.

In emphasizing and seeking to express love, do not overlook other emotions. You can approve and disapprove of behaviors, but not feelings. All feelings are valid, whether they are positive, negative, or neutral, or whether they are felt by children or adults. Recognize and label (but do not judge) feelings for your children. Seek ways of allowing dialogue about feelings, especially seemingly negative ones such as jealousy and anger. Communicate that it is all right to be jealous or angry but not to hit or to break things. Make this a consistent theme. Welcome expression of emotion in acceptable ways while consistently setting limits on unacceptable behaviors.

- Set aside special times for listening to each child's feelings with an open heart and a relatively closed mouth.
- Help the child develop a repertoire of behaviors that are acceptable and attach these behaviors to feelings: "When I am angry I . . . , but I do not . . ."

I have been describing the establishment of an ideal emotional environment in the home—one containing rich, ongoing, and healthy emotional expression for a child. Another extreme of childhood experience is provided by parents who use stony silence as their main way of maintaining control and of expressing or avoiding emotion. These parents create an invisible wall that no one can penetrate. Their children are cut off from emotional contact and, to survive, must learn to do without it. Imagine, hour after hour, day after day, week after week of cold silence coming from one or both of the two most important people in your life. This silence helps shape a child's personality by teaching detachment as a way of life, as a life script. Yet another extreme of childhood experience is provided by parents who regularly resort to physical violence as a means of expressing emotion. Physically abused children can begin to recover from such abuse only when they recognize their parents' behaviors as abuse and when they, usually with help, rebuild their self-esteem and emotional patterns into new forms not based on the molding templates of their family lives.

Emotional contact is an essential part of healthy human development. In fact, many psychologists believe that death can result when too little close contact is provided to a baby. The type of emotional contact a child receives, especially in his or her early years, is an extremely influential part of that child's psychological development. This early emotional training creates lifelong patterns of relating. Whatever the age of the child, love and emotional contact can make a big difference in his or her life and mental development.

Comfort and Security

Communicating to a child in a negative way will lead to negative feelings and behavior. Threatening a child instills fear. Saying "I am ashamed of you" instills guilt. Asking "What is wrong with you?" instills a sense of incompetence, a feeling that something is, indeed, wrong. Don't we all know adults with these traits—negative feelings, fear, guilt, a sense of incompetence?

Of course, there may be times when you raise your voice

with, or your hand to, your children. They are not saints and neither are you. Keep in mind, however, that some of what you say emphatically and loudly can be taken from the list of positive, optimistic messages below. All too often, we tend to be dramatic in our expressions of disappointment, anger, and negativity and too quiet in our expressions of approval, love, and positivity.

Optimism

Consider giving your child positive and optimistic messages about himself or herself. These messages are some of the building blocks of a happy life. Try communicating some of these messages to your child. (Rework these messages into your child's personal vocabulary if that will enable him or her to better understand them.)

- You are wonderful.
- I like you.
- Thank you for being with me, for being in my life.
- You can become anything that you want to be. Your dreams *can* come true.
- You may live to be 100, or more, and do it happily.
- You are in good, terrific, great health.
- You are a contented, satisfied person.
- Add to this list some of the words of approval or affection that you would have like to have heard on a regular basis when you were a kid, and practice saying these words to your child daily.

Clear Communication

One of the most disturbing types of human interaction is unclear communication. Although we are all troubled by vague, and sometimes mixed, messages, children suffer more with these than do the rest of us. Why? Because, psychologically speaking, children are the least likely to say to themselves or to someone else, "That is not clear; I am uncertain as to what is meant by that." Children are the most likely to want to please adults; they seek to either receive love in return or avoid punishment.

You can help your child by editing your comments on an ongoing basis. Of course, we do not always have the presence of mind to think before we speak. But you can *listen* to what you say to your child as you are saying it. If the message is not simple and crystal clear, repeat it until you have gotten it right and then repeat the refined statement a few times in a row.

For example, a parent might say, "Johnny, it's 5 o'clock and I told you to have your room and hands and face clean before dinner and you haven't. So go to your room and do it." This is a lot of message in one statement. The tone in which all of this is spoken is the dominant message: Is the parent angry, disappointed, or simply matter-of-fact? The clarity or lack of clarity is another critical piece of the message: Exactly when is dinner? Does the child still have time? How can the child obey now—how can he wash his hands and face while he is in his room? Be clear. A child should not have to interpret your words for you.

This message must be cleared up. First of all, if the parent is angry or disappointed, the parent should say so. Try, "I am angry because you have not done what I asked you to do." A child should not have the job of trying to interpret a parent's tone of voice. All too often parents combine their own stress and exhaustion with irritation and the need to discipline their children. While this is quite normal, children (of all ages) should be helped to know what emotional elements are present in the voice: "I am also very tired, I had a hard day at work." Second, directions must be clear. "Go to your room and do" exactly what? For how long? Who will say when it is done? Be careful not to give directions that are impossible to follow correctly if followed verbatim, word-for-word. Avoid mixed messages and double binds. Listen to yourself. Are you telling the child that he or she is damned either way? "You didn't do what I asked you and it's too late to do it now." What is the child to do?

Healthy Camaraderie and Social Interaction

We can accept the reality that no family life is entirely harmonious. No family can avoid all tension and disagreement all the time. But every family can aim for as much healthy companionship as possible.

- Create an atmosphere of being on each other's team. Root for your children, cheer them on. Have them root for each other and their parents as well.
- Sit together and enjoy each other. Say that this is what you are doing, that you are spending some time together and enjoying each other, so that children can define the experience.
- Teach your children, by example, to say "hello" and "goodbye," and to look for positive things to say about family members. Encourage positive statements. "Mom, I like your dress." "Cathy, you look pretty today." "You are reading so well now, I'm proud of you." "You did a great job." We can all see something positive in someone else if we learn to look for it.

Interdependence

Need each other. While overdependence can become a problem when it is encouraged, nurtured, or expected, interdependence is healthy. Family members do need each other. Make this clear. "I need some help getting dinner ready." "I need to talk about my day." "I need someone to tell me if my hair looks O.K. from the back."

Identification

Children identify with their families, no matter how extended or how small. Even if you are a single parent of one child, you can build a family consciousness into your child's life—"We are the Smith family." Or, if both parents in the family are using different last names, "We are the Haskin-Smith family." Create a family slogan or song or banner. Establish family traditions. Family identity helps children feel that they have roots, that they have a place on this planet.

Opportunity for Responsibility

As I noted earlier, it was not very long ago in history that children were considered chattel, the property of their parents, primarily of their fathers. The birth of an able-bodied child, especially a male baby, was looked upon as the arrival of two additional wage-earning hands for laboring both at home and at work. Before the enactment of child labor laws, working-class children of what we now call "beginning school age" were put to work for long hours in guilds, factories, and mines.

Quite rightly, we now protect children from such exploitation. Instead, we allow them a childhood. We provide them with formal education. We take care of them in ways unheard of two centuries ago. Yet, in an almost subconscious effort to protect childhood from even the faintest hint of exploitation and from the neglect and abuse associated with it, we sometimes stumble into another form of neglect and of abuse through neglect. This is the neglect to teach responsibility, through chores and participation in the family household.

Why is this form of neglect abusive? Because it creates children who know little about the level of effort or even the type of effort that goes into creating their physical realities. Parents work hard to serve a child: to feed, clothe, drive to school and lessons, pay the rent, and maintain the household. Parents are unsung heroes. But even unsung heroes can neglect to share the responsibility for household chores with their children.

Children who grow up with little participation in the responsibility of maintaining a home and a family are missing out in several ways: They do not learn the essential how-to's of living. They do not feel the pride of contribution. They do not learn responsibility. They do not learn some very practical and essential skills. They grow up expecting to be taken care of. This is a dangerous expectation, one that affects children's school performance. Children expecting to be taken care of do not just drop such expectations in school. They may not request that their teachers baby them, but they often show much less initiative than children who have some sense that they can take care of themselves. Children who do not share in the job of running their households do not develop certain aspects of motivation, self-esteem, and initiative. In school, they do not raise their hands with questions as often or use a dictionary on their own as often as more resourceful children.

Provide your children opportunities to become resourceful, to assume responsibilities. This will have a great impact on their intellectual development. Simple, age-appropriate tasks or chores that can be successfully completed by the child are quite valuable. Successful completion of tasks generates a sense of competence, a feeling of purpose, a sense of importance. In the completing of simple tasks, a child learns that even the most basic projects have beginnings, middles, and ends. The child learns to follow through and assume responsibility, to take the initiative. This learning transfers to other parts of life. The sense of competence and the taking of initiative are essential elements of school success.

Reward Systems

Positive behaviors—however you choose to define them—must be rewarded. The reward can be a hug, a positive statement, the awarding of a privilege, or something material. Match the reward to the behavior being rewarded by degree and by your ability to keep providing the reward. Be careful with monetary rewards. Over time, money provided for every achievement becomes expensive and creates a false expectation that life will consistently pay one for doing well.

Play

I tell parents that, quite often, the best thing to do is to play a lot. This is easy to say, but play what? How? Alone or with others?

Play serves two basic functions. As an "assimilative function," play is a social activity that helps a child to integrate into the society. This is, basically, play with another child or other children in which the children interact. As an "autogenetic function," play is a personal activity that is associated more with individual needs than with those of a social group or society. [3] A child can do this type of play alone or with others, but its developmental effects are more personal than social.

These forms of play need not be mutually exclusive. If play serves both a social and a personal purpose, then developmentally oriented play will encourage both. Because individualization is as much a part of acquiring a social identity as is socialization, play that addresses either of these is, in the end, a social activity. A parent, caregiver, or teacher can encourage both lines of development by providing opportunities for both structured and unstructured play.

Given that play has various forms and serves various purposes, parents do best to encourage many different types of play. Have your children play alone, with friends, and just as importantly, with you. Encourage structured group play in which games or activities are clearly defined (hide-and-seek, foursquare, cards, basketball). Encourage unstructured group activity in which two or more children must deal with each other with a minimum of adult guidance. Encourage quiet reading time and play-alone time, in which a child goes inside his or her own mind for entertainment and stimulation. (This activity should be somewhat mentally engaging, such as playing with dolls or trucks or drawing, not watching television.)

Ritual

Ritual is a special type of structured activity that often incorporates recreation; however, it involves much more than play. Rituals include daily patterns such as meals and bedtimes, arrivals and departures, as well as special celebrations such as birthdays and holidays. The importance of ritual in a child's development is twofold. First, it provides the child with a sense of social patterns—meals occur regularly, naptime is at the same time each day; these are activities that people have in common. Second, rituals, when they are regular observations of special holidays, serve to familiarize the developing child with his or her own culture or subculture, encouraging identification and socialization.

Direct Moral Judgment

Rules and codes of behavior are guidelines for the development of moral judgment. These "guidelines" motivate children to stay within them and to acquire socially acceptable patterns of behavior. The motivation I speak of here is a combination of enforcement (disciplinary action) and reinforcement (approval and affection). As a child matures, morality and moral reasoning grow through a developmental sequence. The earliest stage of moral judgment responds to traditional authoritarian control. The small child does not question or seek to understand authority; such a process would be too intellectually demanding. The later stages of moral judgment, seen in school children as they age, and becoming increasingly apparent as adolescents move into young adulthood, depend on an ability to comprehend the reasons behind the rules. Parents and teachers, therefore, assist the development of moral judgment in a child by teaching not only the rules but the reasons for the rules. The more your child must evaluate his or her own behavior in terms of social and family rules, the more your child must practice moral thinking—and thinking in general.

Developmental Abilities

Daily life offers every member of the family challenges that inspire development. Look for these opportunities for your children. Putting objects away and matching spoons with spoons, blocks with blocks, nuts with nuts, and bolts with bolts are wonderful exercises for a child. These exercises require that a child organize his or her thoughts. Even though the work is with physical objects, as it is being done, mental concepts, ideas, are being mentally manipulated. Look for opportunities in daily life to stimulate your child's mental organization processes. If you are trying to sort paper clips by size, ask your child to help you do so. You can find exercises of this type for children of all ages. Your teenager can help you organize your receipts at tax time. Your 10-year-old can help file your papers. Your 7-year-old can separate unlabeled flower bulbs by type, color, and size.

INTENTIONAL DEVELOPMENT

Beyond the above activities, many of which unfold naturally in daily life, there are many more formal opportunities for the stimulation of your child's mental development. You can plan regular educational activities for your child, including:

- counting and solving mathematical problems together
- doing puzzles
- building models and engines
- visiting museums, nature preserves, and other places of interest
- taking up an educational hobby such as rock or bug collecting
- enrolling in acting, gymnastics, aikido, dance, and/or music lessons

By building specific educational activities into your child's life, beginning at a young age, these activities become an unquestioned, natural part of life. By the time your child is ready to pick and choose his or her own lessons and other educational activities, your child should be used to the fact that such activities are part of life and that the decision is what educational activities should be engaged in rather than whether or not to engage in any. I have found the early start especially helpful when it comes to dance and music lessons. The brain is most open and learns new movements, tones, rhythms, and languages best in the early years.

Family Music

Family music can be mentally, creatively, culturally, and spiritually stimulating. If you play an instrument, do so for and with your child. If you do not, try learning to play. Take music lessons as you have your child do. Consider learning an instrument other than the one your child is studying to avoid parent–child competition. Encourage family performances. Your child will benefit by performing—this builds confidence and concentration "on your feet."

Reading Aloud

Never miss an opportunity to read *to each other*. I emphasize to each other here because, as early as possible, you should have your child share in the reading. Begin by having your child repeat phrases or sentences that you have just read aloud. Then have your child read the easy words in the sentence, pausing and pointing at the easy word each time you come to an "I" or a "the" or an "a" or any word you are reasonably certain that your child knows. Eventually, your child will share the role of family reader—the job of reading aloud. Many parents are thrilled when they realize that their children can read *them* to sleep.

Reading and Working Quietly Together

Institute family quiet times during which all or most members of the immediate family sit in the same area of the house and read, sew, study, draw, or do activities requiring quiet concentration. This model is a behavior that your children will continue through their school years and into their adult lives. Too many modern families have replaced this type of family time with family television watching. Group television watching is an entirely different type of activity than that which I suggest here. It requires less concentration, less spiritual synergy, less togetherness. The physical bodies may sit closely but the hearts and minds tend to go blank, to be much less accessible than when each is reading his or her own book or sewing or drawing quietly nearby.

Role Playing

Good family time is not always quiet. Try role playing. This provides a great opportunity for theatrical and emotional engagement. Have each family member play the role of someone else in the family. You may want to delegate these roles carefully if you have two or more children who are passing through stages of teasing each other. Perhaps they should not play each other, or perhaps they should, but only with prestated rules.

Et Cetera

Develop your own stimulating family activities. As you become increasingly sensitive to your children's needs to identify with their family, and to see good uses of time modeled by family members, you will discover your own ways of meeting these needs.

COUNTERINTELLIGENCE IN THE FAMILY

While there is a great deal that families can do to enhance the intelligence of their children, there is just as much that families can do to detract from or discourage their children's intelligence. We tend to overlook the many discouragements to intellectual thinking that are present in our children's lives. I will describe just a few of these here.

Family Disorganization

Family disorganization is a form of counterintelligence. This is a family management issue. If your family life feels disorganized, do not assume that something is wrong with you or your marriage or your family. You are sharing an experience with millions of modern families, most of whom need training in family management.

Family management is a psychological as well as a practical problem. The psychological state of parents is affected by the ease with which they feel they can manage their family lives and vice versa. When both parents work away from the home full time, they require advanced family management skills to meet sanely and effectively the doubled demands of parenting and of working for pay. When neither parent has a spouse at home who serves as full-time homemaker and family manager, the void has to be filled. Someone has to find the time to prepare the dinner, to buy the food, and to clean the dishes. Effective management is the key.

Although the economic status of a family determines its ability to afford a wide range of consumer goods and services, it says little about the family's ability to organize its time and energy. Scheduling and planning are challenges for most families, regardless of income. In fact, when parents work long hours out of the home, the last thing they have energy for is scheduling further responsibilities. But scheduling can end up saving energy. A family's ability to arrange time to shop, to commute, to be involved in community activities, to know the next-door neighbors, to prepare meals and to eat them, and, most importantly, to be together are products of good family management.

Without time for it, parents do very little parenting, spouses do very little sharing, people do very little caring. Too many working parents live in a perpetual time crunch in which home serves as a station for sleeping, eating, paying bills, and changing clothes. When relationships between family members are caught in this crunch, people who actually love and care very much about each other start to grind away at each other. It seems that many people find it is easier to be distant or irritable on the fly than to express good feeling in passing. Scheduling time for good feeling, as whimsical as it may sound, is essential. Somehow, too many of us made it into adulthood without learning to make and stick to workable family plans. We must show our children that it is possible to have time to be a family and to feel like one.

Family management is difficult for most working parents. Employed, married female parents average 40 hours each week at work, 20 hours each week on home chores, and 25 hours each week on child care. Employed, married male parents with employed wives average 44 hours each week on employment, 11 hours each week on home chores, and 14 hours each week on child care. Many women I have spoken with about these averages claim that their husbands put in fewer hours than listed here while they, the working wives, put in more hours than I have listed here. They also tell me that "My husband does less at home than I do even though I spend more hours at the office than he does." "I assume full responsibility for the kids even though my husband and I both work full time." These are not uncommon reports.

Comparing the totals of the numbers listed above: women spend 85 hours a week on a combination of employment, home chores, and child care, while their husbands' total is 69 hours each week. If an individual has 16 waking hours each day, or 112 waking hours a week, these working women have 27 hours left after these responsibilities, while their husbands have 43 hours left. And commute time, time with one's spouse, and time for community involvement, such as PTA meetings, have not been added in here. How much "free" time do working parents of either sex really have? When free time is so limited, only careful planning creates time for the family.

What all this boils down to is this: The only way to incorporate my suggestions into your children's lives and into their mental developments, is to *plan to do so*. Write a weekly schedule that includes the suggestions in this chapter and others. Create a family reading time if you do not have one. Create official study times if they do not exist. Plan times to work with your children

on the concentrated aspects of mental development I offer in
Chapters 9 through 12 of this book. Select items from the other
chapters that you want to emphasize and schedule them into your
lives. Many parents use an appointment book, kept in the com-
munal living area, in which they write these activities. Write your
family schedule your own way, but do it. Older children can help
or even take charge of the planning. Fight the counterintelligence
of family disorganization.

Sib Order Biases

Here is another, very different form of what I call counterintelligence in the family. Parents of more than one child cannot
help but compare their children. Quite often, parents observe
differences in mental ability, frequently noting that it is the
firstborn child who seems brighter. They often ask, "Why is my
first child brighter and more successful than my second child?
Have I failed my second child or are first children naturally better
at things? Is there anything I can do for my second-born?"
(Whenever I say "second-born" here, I am referring to any child
who was born after another sibling. This could be a third-,
fourth-, or fifth-born as well.)

Whether or not we find our firstborns brighter, many of us
fall into a couple of very uncomfortable cultural traps. The first
trap is the use of the word "better" in describing our children.
Thinking in terms of "better" and "worse" oversimplifies people.
Whenever we compare two people in a simple way, one will come
out seeming to be more or less than the other. People are not
simple beings. They cannot be compared simply. And children
are people, too.

The second trap is one in which being brighter and more
successful is equated with being better. Break this equation by
dropping the emphasis on "better." Being brighter and more

successful does not necessarily have anything to do with being better. Many bright and successful people are better at some things and worse at others. Let go of this connection.

When it is the firstborn who seems to lead intellectually, to be the better thinker or the higher achiever, we must be aware of the difficulty experienced by the second- and later-born children. Firstborn children tend to be hard acts to follow for their younger siblings. "Sib order," the order in which children are born into a family, has a profound influence on children's perceptions of themselves. Firstborns tend to feel more confident and in control. And, quite often, but definitely not always, firstborn children are higher achievers in school and exhibit more leadership characteristics than second-born children. When they do so, firstborns then tend to carry these childhood characteristics on into adulthood, achieving and leading in adult life.

This is not to say that second-born children do not do well in life. In many cases they catch up to their firstborn brothers and sisters as they differentiate from them. Parents can encourage this differentiation process by creating opportunities for second-born children to develop in areas in which the firstborn children are not actively involved. Sisters and brothers need not compete to be better than each other. They can enjoy their differences. (This is, of course, somewhat easier if the siblings are not of the same gender—the competition is somewhat less in this case.)

All too often, second-born children are expected to follow in the footsteps of firstborn children. Sometimes second-born children rebel. They develop a new role for themselves. As one second-born explained, "My brother was always the best kid in the family and the best at school. So the only way I could be different was to be very bad and very stupid. He got all the positive attention—so I took what was left."

Every family is different and, therefore, every second-born has a different experience. Sometimes the firstborn gets into a lot of trouble and the second-born is able to differentiate by being the "good kid."

Another way families differ is in the age differences between their children. The more years between children, the greater the probability that each will have the firstborn type of experience. Children who are seven years or more apart will rarely if ever view themselves as occupying the same developmental territory. They thus compete less with their siblings.

Generally speaking, parents' direct influence on firstborns is greater than on the second-borns. Because they have only one child to parent at the beginning of the firstborn's life, their parenting energy is enthusiastic and undivided. Parents' expectations and desires for the success of their firstborns are more clearly transmitted. Firstborns tend to take in, to "internalize," the level of drive and ambition that their parents have for them. They may also internalize any pressure to achieve that they feel. When the second child comes on the scene, parents' attentions are divided and, often, they are strained. Parental drive and ambition may have already been passed on to the firstborn. Something else may get expressed to the second-born. The message, no matter how hard parents may try to avoid sending it, is often heard by the second-born as "fit in to this already established family. Take your place in line."

Parents are right to be concerned that their second-borns get second best. Yet parents need not view themselves as failing their second-borns. It is important to make it clear that your parental love and optimism is not merit based. Children who are not high achievers, whatever their birth order, need as much parental love and support as children who are achievers. Children who are not high achievers also need to feel that their parents are as optimistic about their futures as they are about the futures of high achievers.

Parents must also be sensitive to the effect that a firstborn's dominance due to seniority has upon the second-born. Second-borns are as strongly affected by disapproval coming from first-borns as they are by a lack of perceived parental love and support. The firstborn has a loving parent or two all to himself for a while. The second-born has a loving parent or two whom she must always share with a sibling who is not necessarily loving. This situation can interfere with mental development.

Watch sibling relationships closely. Brothers' and sisters' behaviors can be much more damaging to children than their parents' behaviors. Do not force your second-born on your first-born or vice versa. Let the children find each other when they are ready. Parenting is a question of balance. Parents are jugglers. Professional circus jugglers will tell you just how important timing is.

Credit yourself for the good things that you do for your children and that they do for themselves. Give each of your children approval aimed specifically at his or her individual qualities on a regular basis, and give yourself some as well. Approval is a great vitamin. It nourishes the soul.

Television

Television, that electronic babysitter, permanent house guest, and technological hybrid in-law, is the ultimate in counterintelligence when used in excess. Why do our children beg us for it as if it were water in a drought-parched desert? Why do our children become oblivious to all around them, even their favorite toys and loving parents, when the TV is on? What is it about that dull glow that attracts them so, even when the sun is most brilliantly lighting the world outside?

Television is practically a family member. Television is *easy*. Even a toddler can turn it on, change the channel, and turn it off. Television is *undemanding*. A child can sit there, as numb as can be, and be entertained. There is no need for the viewer to think at all, even when the program being watched purports itself to be educational or, using a new buzzword, *interactive*. Television is *ever present*. Whereas parents become dull with fatigue, get distracted by responsibility, and are called away to telephones or appointments, television never gets exhausted or busy or called away and is there with a flick of the switch. Television is *entertaining*. Even when the content is not entirely exciting, there is the color, the noise, and the perpetual motion. This sure beats parents—they tend to be dull, sit still, look tired and pale, and have little to say sometimes. Television is a *passive stimulus*—no interaction necessary. Are children stimulus junkies? Have we addicted the next generation to an electronic breast? Have we adults led the way for our children with our own television-viewing behavior?

Yet before we take our televisions to the garage and hammer them to bits, we must remember that excessive use of almost anything is unhealthy. Television, in moderation and with the guidance I advise below, can actually be a valuable addition to a child's life. I am, therefore, an advocate of controlled use of television. Television should be a supplement to life, not a substitute for it.

By "controlled use" I mean nonaddicted use, not unlimited, unhealthy use, that is, use to the exclusion of other important developmental activities such as reading, drawing, play, exercise, helping around the house, and doing homework well, not racing through it. What might this use look like? Parents must guide this use:

- Communicate in practice and in words from birth on that *television watching is a restricted activity*, the amount to be determined by the parent. The earlier you begin implanting this concept in the child's mind, the easier it will be to maintain it as the child grows.
- Restrict television watching to a consistent number of hours a week. For school-age children, I suggest no more than eight hours, with the television viewing occurring only on days when there is no school. (Television is on at least six hours a *day* in the typical American household.) [4] Preschool-age children have slightly different needs.

Studies have shown that a certain amount of television viewing can actually be developmentally stimulating for preschool-age children but that after about ten hours per week, the effects of television viewing wane and become negative. What this means is that a little television can be good, a little more is less so, and a lot more is bad. Families with whom I have worked found that their children's television watching, in the face of the explicit limits I list here, drops to an average of four to six hours a week (including videos) during the school year and eight hours a week when school is out. I stress "averages" here, because I find that visits to friends' houses where limits to television watching are not practiced increase the weekly total. I also suggest that parents find subtle ways of sticking to or coming in below the desired average by creating activities that leave no time for television.

- Include videotape watching and educational television in the total. Video is, after all, an image coming through the television screen. This holds for educational videos as well.
- Remember to maintain control over the type of program being watched. This holds for children of all ages. Cartoons, no matter how socially valuable or educational, should be limited. I avoid any programming with commercials. Commercials are a brainwashing process, planting a "buy me" demand in the minds of children. Commercials are a poor use of your child's brain time. Educational programs dealing with nature, building, science, mathematics, geography, painting, and even cooking are wonderful, even for young children who may not understand all of what they hear.
- Restrict parental watching to evenings past your child's bedtime or to a room away from the central part of the house. Parents need not follow the same rules as children: parents' brains are past the extremely vulnerable stage. I

nevertheless believe that many adults dull their minds with television overuse. A parent with a television-deadened mind cannot be intellectually stimulating to a child.

The child is in the family environment for a significant amount of his or her lifetime. Parents can make this environment stimulating or dulling, secure or threatening, organized or chaotic. Take your choice. You are in charge here.

Chapter 8

The Child in the Physical Environment

my desk

MY Room

123

No one was coming. No one ever did come, it seemed, and she took another long breath, because she could not help it, and she held back the swinging curtain of ivy and pushed back the door which opened slowly—slowly. Then she slipped through it, and shut it behind her, and stood with her back against it, looking about her and breathing quite fast with excitement, and wonder, and delight. She was standing *inside* the secret garden.
—Frances Hodgson Burnett,
The Secret Garden

From birth right on through adolescence, the child's physical environment plays a critical although often unheralded role in the development and expression of his or her intelligence. This chapter therefore focuses briefly on some of the important physical characteristics of an intelligence-promoting environment. Whether the child is at home, at school, at preschool, or somewhere else, many specific characteristics of the surroundings have a profound influence on the structuring of the child's thinking processes.

The belief that an environment can actually be intelligence promoting is often agreed upon, but is, just as often, treated lightly. We must always have our eyes highly attuned to the particular and often hidden effects of the physical environment on the development and expression of intelligence. So many opportunities are missed when we overlook detail.

Examine the places where your child spends the most time. This is likely to be home and school or preschool. As a parent, you have the greatest say in the nature of the home environment. If you are a teacher, you have the classroom to design as an intelligence-promoting environment.

You may note that, as elsewhere in this book, several of the subsections in this chapter refrain from pinpointing a particular age group. This is because much of what follows applies to children and young people of all ages. In fact, particular aspects of the physical environment, such as its organization, clutter, color, and safety, also influence the workings of adults' minds. Throughout this book, I use the word "child" to refer to anyone younger than you who is in some way dependent on you, primarily children from birth through the age of 18. Before turning to specific intelligence-enhancing characteristics of the physical environment, let us focus briefly on two basic physical prerequisites of any form of mental ability, the nutrition of the body and the development of the brain.

NUTRITION IS AN ISSUE

Food is a key aspect of the child's physical environment. Nutrition is the bridge between a child's physical surroundings and his or her body. All physical and mental development is dependent on nutritional intake. Without food, the organism dies. Parents and educators must not only understand dietary requirements of young children and the developmental processes that depend on nutrition but also be certain that children get enough of the right foods to eat. Toddlers from 1 to 3 years old need between 900 and 1,800 calories daily. Children from 4 to 6 need between 1,300 and 2,300 calories daily. Older children usually require between 2,000 and 3,000 calories a day, depending on how physically active they are, their rates of growth, and, if they are in late adolescence, whether or not they are still growing at all. [1] What are the right foods? A balance of fruits and vegetables and whole grains and enough protein and water are the right foods. There are many ways to put a proper diet together.

Consult modern (not outdated) books on nutrition or a doctor for detailed advice.

A word about the wrong foods. The way we nourish the developing mind from birth right on through to the age of 18 is critical. Childhood is a time when foods with sugar, caffeine, and theobromine (chocolates) are tasted and frequently consumed in large quantities. These mind-affecting, mood-distorting, "psychoactive" compounds are provided by adults who either cannot say no or do not understand that children can develop sugar, caffeine, and theobromine dependencies. In some cases, parents actually use these dietary drugs—the psychoactive compounds found in food and beverages—to control their children. "If you are good, I'll buy you a candy bar," or "If you eat all of your dinner, you can have cake for dessert," or "Get ready for bed and you can have some ice cream."

When parents complain, "My children just won't calm down enough to go to bed without their ice cream," they are revealing the fact that their children have become dependent on the effects of sugar on their young bodies in order to calm down. In many children, sugar causes a brief increase in energy, followed by the calming release of serotonin in the brain accompanied by a depressive drop in blood-sugar levels.

Poor nutrition, including the intake of dietary and other drugs, is as much a form of counterintelligence as is the excessive television watching discussed in Chapter 7. As children grow older, they see their parents eating poorly, and often smoking, drinking, and using various drugs. Then they see and hear countless advertisements showing happy and attractive people eating sugar-filled foods, smoking cigarettes, and drinking alcohol. Given that children are born and raised in this chemically dependent society, it is not surprising that they face the risk of becoming chemically dependent as adolescents and, later on, as adults. Almost every one of us has been influenced in some way by the high use of dietary and nondietary, legal and illegal drugs—our own use and that of the encompassing society.

Adolescents and even adults feel social or peer pressure to "do what everyone else is doing," to "fit in," and, at an increasingly younger age in this competitive society, to "keep up." Especially among preteens and teenagers, the desire not to stand out as being odd or different may be the prime motivation to experiment with and even regularly use alcohol and other drugs. The sense of social pressure begins at a tragically early age. Unfortunately, the younger the child is when he or she first experiments with both legal and illegal drugs, the greater the likelihood that he or she will have trouble with drugs later on. [2]

Let us relate this predicament to the nutrition of the body. Families struggle with their children's and teenagers' desires to experiment with drugs and to respond to media and peer pressure. Yet they often undermine their own struggles by simultaneously creating the poor nutritional standards and types of dietary intake that render young people susceptible to biological cravings for drugs. After all, a childhood of high-sugar consumption can program a young person's body to accept chemically induced highs and lows. Using drugs such as alcohol, marijuana, and cocaine to achieve highs and lows later on in life is simply to switch drugs or to add another drug to the list of those already being taken in through the diet. The chemicals may be different, but the process is exactly the same.

MYELINIZING THE BRAIN

Physical development is often regarded as something that must be visible to be happening. We assume that children must be getting taller and more muscular, maturing in facial characteristics, improving in coordination, if physical development is taking place. However, beneath the visible surface of the child's body, many internal developments are also occurring.

Among these developments are the massive and essential changes in the brain and nervous system that occur in childhood. "Myelinization," the process of coating or sheathing particular nerve fibers in a fatty substance called *myelin*, is incomplete in infancy. During early infancy and early childhood, myelinization proceeds most rapidly. Significant myelinization is also believed to occur between the ages of 6 and 10, when the corpus callosum (which connects the nerve fibers of the right and left hemispheres) is completed, as are the parietal and frontal areas of the cortex, the outer layer of the brain. Some myelinization is believed to continue in certain parts of the brain until at least the age of 30.

The intensive myelinization process, which occurs only in the higher regions of the brain, affects learning, the development of language and memory, and the control of impulses. Analytic and spatial abilities may be connected where specialized regions of the brain are linked by myelinized nerves. [3] Where myelinization fails to occur, learning and other disabilities may ensue. Where myelinization is maximized, the mental capacity of the child's brain is maximized. Other nervous system changes linked to this type of brain development include the speeding up and structuring of the brain waves, the changing of sleep patterns during childhood, and fine motor and hormonal developments. All of these less visible physical developments accompany the development of gross motor skills (including walking and running) during childhood. All these neuromuscular and mental developments reflect the process of myelinization, that is, neural connection within the brain.

What is it about the physical environment that gives direct impetus to myelinization of the brain? Physical activity, proper nutrition, and the right stimulation from the physical environment are essential. Many aspects of the environment to which we might not be attentive affect mental development. For example, experiments have demonstrated that the "blink response" (normally beginning early in infancy) develops an average of three weeks earlier in young infants who have been regularly provided with a stable visual pattern over their cribs on which to focus (for at least one-half hour a day). [4] There have been numerous studies that report the negative effects of a deprived, unstimulating environment on development. [5] Basically stated, the mental development of children who are not stimulated by their physical environments is poor. The mental development of children who are stimulated by their physical environments is rich. We must, therefore, pay close attention to particular and often overlooked aspects of a young person's environment. I discuss some of the aspects below.

ORGANIZATION

Of all the physical characteristics of a child's environment, organization is one of the most critical. This does not mean that children need an extremely organized environment. It does mean that a certain level of organization is important and that a child feels the effects of this organization in many ways:

- A child who knows where to find most of his or her shoes, shirts, and other regularly needed items most of the time feels secure about this and benefits from this security.
- A child who knows that there is a neat, organized area in the house where he or she can do homework each day, and can count on this, will be more likely to return to that spot again and again.
- A child who studies in a neat, organized spot will concentrate better, work more neatly, and complete more work.
- When a child regularly experiences organization in his or her physical environment, that child's mind adapts to this

reality in subtle ways. The internal mental environment—the mind—of the child mimics the external environment: *An organized mind reflects an organized environment.* This is especially true as the child matures and becomes increasingly involved in maintaining the organization of the living space. "Keeping the place neat" becomes a psychological as well as a physical practice.

When a child contributes to the organization of the physical space in which he or she lives and works, there are many positive effects, including the following:

- A sense of control over the environment grows within the child. Increasing mastery of the physical environment spills over into an increasing sense of mastery over his or her psychological (feeling) and cognitive (thinking) environments.
- The child's efforts to organize objects in the physical outer world serve as valuable training for the organizing of thoughts in the mental inner world.
- An ongoing sense of accomplishment is generated. With that sense comes a feeling that all kinds of tasks, even challenging ones, can indeed be accomplished.

The experience of organization and the participation in the creating of organization are essential to the realization of a child's mental potential. There is a security in organization, a security that relieves tension and allows the child the emotional space to develop. As was once explained to me by a child who lived in a household undergoing extreme disorganization due to the stress of sick grandparents and a seriously injured parent: "Chaos is exotic. It's strange 'cuz it's not usual. It makes little children trip and fall. It makes some big kids act wild." (I was surprised at her use of the word "exotic." It is an unusual word for a 6-year-old child, which was her age at the time.)

FREEDOM

Freedom to explore the surrounding space provides essential stimulation to a child's mind. For very young children, the space with which you must be most concerned is the immediate home and child-care environment. As children grow, their space expands—to another floor of the house, the yard, friends' homes, school, and the neighborhood. With adolescents being so mobile these days, your entire community, town, or city (and maybe even state) must be examined. Children and young persons need freedom to explore their spaces at all ages. You need the security of knowing what they are exploring.

So be certain that the child's physical environment offers as much freedom as possible. First, take care of all safety issues in an age-appropriate way (for example, baby gates for crawling and toddling children, matches hidden from children until they are at least 10 years old, alcohol out of reach and sight of adolescents). Once you have addressed safety issues, define the areas in the home, yard, neighborhood, and even city (for your older children) that you will permit the child to explore. Try to communicate that you are providing freedom rather than taking it away.

RESOURCES

Among the details that should be included in a child's environment are learning resources. These resources should, for the most part, be available for use without needing an adult to "reach them," "take them out," or "find them." All children should have ready access to writing utensils and paper. Keep crayons within reach for the young ones and pens, pencils, and pencil sharpeners for school-age children. Children who have begun to read and spell will need a dictionary. Older children should have access to encyclopedias as well. As of about 5 years of age, a typewriter or computer is valuable. Now that we have entered the age of the computer, children will need typing skills for the rest of their lives. They may as well start young. All children will benefit from color charts, templates for drawing shapes, art supplies, and other drawing and crafting resources.

Again, taking age into consideration, keep these resources within the child's reach so that the child may use them without asking for help to do so. When a child can use resources on his or her own initiative, without an adult making it possible, a child can initiate a private, self-directed learning experience at will.

GUIDANCE

Parents, teachers, and other involved adults serve as guides to the world, especially the physical world. What this means is that adults show children "how to be" in a museum, in a library, in a forest, on a cliff, in a toy store, and so on. Beginning at an early age, take the role of "guide" on this visit to "planet Earth" with your child.

After having shown the way, you must consciously aim to become at times a follower. This is increasingly so as the child ages. Encourage your child to lead you as often as possible. For example, let a child take you on a tour of a forest or botanical garden. Let a child show you around the neighborhood or around his or her room.

COLOR

Children are very sensitive to color. Attitude, tension level, attention span, and creativity are all influenced by the colors we see around us. This makes our choice and use of color much more important than we tend to think it is.

Color choice involves the sensitive selection and arrangement of different colors in a room as well as an awareness of the contrasts among the colors used. Young children are actually more aware of *contrasts between colors* than the specific colors. When my daughter was a baby, the room in our house that had served as my office became her nursery. I had decorated my office in black and white a few years before she was born, and bits of that color scheme survived my painting the walls a rich pink and the trim a bright sky blue. The result was a black and white and blue and pink room. I was astounded to find that the first parts of her room that held her visual attention were the black-and-white curtains and pillows, not the items and walls that were rich pink and vivid blue. I later realized that the pink and blue I had chosen, when translated into gray tones, were of exactly the same value. As different as these colors appeared to be in my eyes, they provided little contrast to each other in my infant daughter's eyes. In a black-and-white photo of the room, they looked to be about the same shade of gray. You can test your own use of color contrast by taking black-and-white photos of the rooms you live in or of the rooms you are decorating and of samples of the colors with which you plan to decorate.

Use color contrast and color itself to create feelings of security and relaxation within a space and to invite notice and enjoyment of an environment. As your own children mature, give them increasing say as to the colors they wear and see (in their bedrooms). Use your judgment and say "no" whenever you feel that you must. I remember a boy about 6 years of age who wanted his room painted black because, as he said, "It would make space more interesting." His parents, who did not like the idea, compromised. They painted one of his walls black. He later surprised them by decorating that wall as a scene from outer space.

DETAIL BUT NOT CLUTTER

Detail is essential in a child's environment. However, let us now confuse clutter with detail. As I have said elsewhere, the physical environment should be organized and not chaotic. It should offer many attractive details of interest. The detail should be appealing, stimulating, and orderly, as well as hygienic and safe.

HEALTHY PHYSICAL SURROUNDINGS

Especially during early childhood, the stage of life when physical growth is most accelerated, the quality of the physical environment is critical. It is in providing a sound physical environment that parents protect, nurture, and develop the bodies of their children. Remember, the body houses the brain and affects mental development.

Physical protection involves a focus on basic health matters, including:

- Efforts to spot any disabilities or ailments a child may have, and to see a doctor when a diagnosis is needed.
- Awareness of the degree of contagion associated with particular illnesses being "passed around" at preschool or school and in the neighborhood. The likelihood of contagion among large groups of unrelated children who spend long hours together in relatively small spaces (such as day-care rooms or classrooms) increases in crowded settings. This is because general upkeep, cleanliness, and sanitation are much more difficult to sustain in overpopulated environments than they are in the relatively less crowded living space we call "home." In day care, preschool, and school,

time-pressed caregivers and teachers may fail to separate infected children from the group and may overlook procedures such as hand washing.

Never enough concern can be directed at the safety of a child-care environment. Toys, equipment, building designs, and nearby streets or parking lots all represent potential dangers to children. The physical environment must be regulated and constantly monitored for safety. Parents who seek to evaluate the physical environments of their children's preschools and schools will want to examine the following:

- The condition of the surrounding neighborhood, its safety, the level of noise, and the pollution.
- The square footage of indoor and outdoor areas in terms of adequate space per child.
- The condition of a cafeteria or kitchen, the toilets, the bathing facilities, the equipment, and the supplies.
- The safety of the grounds, accesses, and equipment.
- The means of controlling indoor air quality, such as heating, cooling, and ventilation.
- The aesthetics and comfort of the physical surroundings.
- The extent to which physical surroundings provide an opportunity for privacy, a sense of order, and a stimulating experience.
- The degree to which the environment invites safe learning, thinking, and concentration.

EKISTICS

Space, time patterns, things, and people are tangible elements of the child's environment. Do an experiment. Consciously make yourself "see" these things everywhere you go for about one month. You will find that you see so much more than you did before, even when you are not thinking of doing so. You will have trained yourself to have an "ekistic" awareness.

You may have had this experience as the parent of a toddler. You may have instinctively trained yourself to find—to see—all of the dangers to a roaming toddler in every new environment you entered. Maybe you would just walk through a doorway and see knives, razor blades, electrical equipment, dangerous toys, breakable objects, items that could be swallowed, and other things you would never have noticed before and might not be so prone to notice a few years later. If you found this happening to you, your ekistic awareness had been developed in a certain way out of your desire to protect your child.

Adults who select, provide, organize, and design the physical surroundings of children would do well to develop a strong ekistic awareness. A child's environment influences his or her activities. This is the work of "spatial forces," as they are called in the terminology of ekistics. All spatial forces are either directional or nondirectional. Directional forces attract or repel. For example, the front of a classroom, a family dinner table, a large tree, or a playground fence attracts or constrains the physical activity of adults and children in the vicinity. Nondirectional forces do not attract or repel but have other sensory effects. These forces include the size of a room, the proportions of a building, and the textures of some upholstery. Each of these spatial forces affects behavior within its physical space. [6] Study corners and special places for particular possessions are also important. From an ekistic perspective, the child's environment should have special areas for which particular activities are consistently designated, such as a dining area, a sleeping area, a work table, and a place to dress.

If your child is old enough to be "out and about," look at your neighborhood and community from an ekistic perspective. Do you see open spaces where one can run freely? Police cars providing a sense of security or of being watched, patrolled? "No trespassing" or "danger" signs? A safe or dangerous town square? Take a walk, ride a bike, take a bus, go cruising in your car, or get around town the way your child would. See the world through his or her eyes. Get to know the ekistic reality in which people of your child's age live. We can begin to set realistic boundaries only when we understand the space we seek to limit.

Mental development, ranging from the forming of neural connections within the brain to the development of healthy psychological reactions to anxiety and the generating of a sense of security, is guided, nourished, and empowered by exploration of the physical world. Adults bring children into and then guide them through physical reality. The experiences we give children—the nutrition, protection, stimulation, organization, freedom, and exploration—are reflected in the functioning of their minds.

Chapter 9

Developing Children's Mental Abilities

a.star.

a star is to Beycome a wundrft
w theing and wen it is day
one star Remans. It is the sun
But wen it is night
one ziulin miuun stars in the
sky.

Chapter. two

We have a star It is
the sun It is too Bright for us

"How is the plan coming, Charlotte? Have you got very far with it? . . . Wilbur was trembling again, but Charlotte was cool and collected.

"Oh, it's coming all right," she said, lightly. "The plan is still in its early stages and hasn't completely shaped up yet, but I'm working on it."

"When do you work on it?" begged Wilbur.

"When I'm hanging head-down at the top of my web. That's when I do my thinking, because then all the blood is in my head."

—Wilbur the pig and Charlotte the spider,
in *Charlotte's Web* by E. B. White

Children develop what I have described as mental abilities under almost any circumstance. Yet parents and teachers can make a significant difference in the degree to which children realize their mental potentials. How?

- By recognizing that you, as parent or teacher, have a great influence upon the development of your child's mind.
- By believing that you can help raise your child's mental ability.
- By letting your child know, from the start (even if you believe that your child is too young to understand), that you *value* mental ability.
- By helping your child develop an awareness of his or her own mental activity.
- By teaching your child that everyone can learn and that learning is an ongoing process.
- By taking an active role in your child's mental development.

In this chapter, I discuss some methods of taking an active role in the mental development of your child. These include teaching strategy selection, encouraging verbal ability, teaching spatial skills, developing number skills, using music in learning, emphasizing organizational skills, recognizing differences, learning relativity, heightening concentration, strengthening memory, and increasing sheer brain speed.

TEACH STRATEGY SELECTION

Communicate the importance of selecting a strategy. Again, we must ask children to consider the existence of a level of thinking above just thinking directly about the subject or issue at hand. The concept, even the word "strategy," may be too complex to ask a child to learn; however, you can teach a child to think about the concept of problem-solving strategy, even from an early age. In fact, if you begin mentioning strategy from the age of 3, and slowly increase the complexity of your comments about strategy, your child will become quite accustomed to the word and the concept and incorporate it into his or her own world view. Just talking about strategy paves the way for a greater understanding of it.

We can start to teach strategy in short little lessons during the early years. Consider this conversation I had with a first grader. My notes about the conversation are in italics.

> "If I ask you what seven take away two is, how do you get the answer?" (*I presented the problem to be solved.*)
> "Well, I go: one plus one is two, and one plus one plus one is three, and one plus one plus one plus one is four, and one plus one plus one plus one plus one is five, and five plus one plus one is seven." (*She uses her fingers but does not look at them.*)
> "So, then, what is seven take away two?"
> "Five."

"Right. How did you get that?" (*This "how" is asking about the strategy the child used.*)

"Because if six is after five and seven is after six, then if you take two away, the seven and the six, you get five." (*Interesting method.*)

"Good. So what was your strategy?" (*Here is my chance to use the word "strategy."*)

"What strategy?" (*Great! She asked!*)

"Strategy is the way you figure something out."

"Once Julia's cat said, 'Mickey.'" (*Her mind wanders.*)

"Oh, her cat can talk. I like it when a cat talks. So strategy is how you figure something out." (*I come back to my point.*)

"Yeah."

"So what strategy did you use to get the answer to seven take away two?" (*I want more on the strategy.*)

"I used my head."

"I thought you counted on your fingers." (*I dig for more information.*)

"No I didn't, I went like this." (*She looked away from her hands while bending her fingers back one by one.*)

"O.K. So, what would you say that strategy is? Using your head while using your fingers while you think?" (*I say this slowly.*)

"Yeah. One plus one plus one."

"So do your fingers help?"

"No. My fingers do not help."

"So what do your fingers do when you do that?"

"It just . . . it just feels good on my fingers."

"And do the fingers help you keep track of what you are thinking, even when you don't look at them?"

"No. No, they do not. They help me feel sure." (*So moving fingers is part of the strategy. They help her feel sure.*)

"Sure of what?"

"Sure of the numbers I am thinking about."

"O.K. Let's try another problem. What is seven take away three?" (*I introduce another problem as a way of extending strategy past the first example.*)

"Seven take away three is four." (*She answers quickly.*)

"How did you do that?"

"I just did it. I didn't have to count, because I'm in first grade and you know more things in first grade than you do in kindergarten." (*Sheer memory is used here. No obvious strategy.*)

"And what about six take away three?" (*She thinks a little longer.*)

"Uh . . . it's three. Let's see . . . Six take away three is three."

"Right. And how did you get that one?"

"Three plus three is six, so six take away three is three."

"Oh, so you added first and then subtracted." (*This is a strategy.*)

"Yes, I knew the adding part already but not the subtracting part."

"But on seven take away three you knew the answer right off."

"Yes, I've known it since I was a baby."

"You remembered it."

"I said I knew it when I was a baby."

"It sounds as if you used a different strategy for each problem I gave you today." (*I introduce the idea that there is more than one strategy for solving a particular type of problem.*)

"What's a strategy?" (*Good. We come back to strategy.*)

"It's the way you solve a problem. You can remember the answer to seven take away three. You can add three plus three to get six, and then you can figure out what six take away three is. You can count in your head while using your fingers but not looking at them to get seven take away two. So what do you think strategy is?"

"I think it's when, um . . . um, like when my friend's dad did it on my puzzle." (*She gives an example.*)

"Ah. What did he do? Solve a hard puzzle?"

"Yes."

"Did he have a strategy?"

"Yes."

"What was his strategy?"

"He put the puzzle pieces behind the other ones that would go in the same place and if the first ones didn't work, he tried more and if the second ones didn't work, then tried the next ones." (*So she seems to understand that strategy is the method used to solve a problem.*)

"So strategy is the way you think about something when you're trying to figure it out." (*I summarize.*)

"Yeah."

I stopped there and we went back to the matter of the talking cat. Keep your discussion of strategy to the point. If the child's mind wanders once or twice, bring it back. If it wanders five or more times, phase out the session and come back to the topic again later.

You do not have to teach all there is to know about strategy in one sitting. In fact, do not try. Over the years your conversations will become more and more sophisticated. Your children will become increasingly conscious of their uses of mental strategies as you continue to talk to them about such uses.

ENCOURAGE VERBAL ABILITY

Encourage the child to participate in discussions. Talk to him or her about ideas, about how things work, about what things mean, about anything you can talk about in a low-pressure, friendly situation. Remember that a discussion is not a monologue. A child learns by listening to you but also by teaching his or her ideas to you:

- by explaining functions (how and why things work)
- by giving definitions (what words mean and how they are used)
- by describing processes (what leads to what and under what circumstances)

Remember that no explanation that requires thinking and creativity is ever entirely wrong. Get your child used to putting thoughts into words.

Give your child words to put thoughts into and words that will stimulate thinking. Introduce new words such as "strategy," "complex," "abstract," "fragile," "absurd," "chaotic," and any other words that come to your mind. Keep a notebook to help you remember what words you are introducing. Understand that it may take years for a child to really master the use of a complex word. You have time. Begin as young as you can, and remember, if you did not start early, it is never too late to begin. Expand your child's vocabulary potential. Begin when the child is very young—when he or she still says "ga-ga da-da." Say lists of polysyllabic words in sets that share a similar sound, such as "fabulous, hazardous, wondrous, tremendous, stupendous." As the child ages, help the child slowly repeat these words. Stimulate clear thought.

ENCOURAGE EXPLANATIONS
OF HOW THE WORLD WORKS

Listen carefully. If the child's explanations are not entirely correct, help the child reformulate them, but do it gently. I discuss the process of reformulation in depth in Chapter 11. Here, I focus on the general character of the process. Ease the child into a revision of his or her understanding of the particular function, definition, or process you think is incorrect. Do not demand that the child just change his or her mind. Do not criticize or reprimand a child for his or her incorrect information. Do not say, for example, "No, a car does not run on air and that's that," or "No, you're wrong, a 'constant' is not a flying star, that's a 'comet,'" or "No, the sun does not turn off when it goes down, it goes to the other side of the Earth." Try to avoid flat, blunt, abrupt corrections. Unless such corrections are delivered with the utmost care, they can have negative effects. Children can feel frowned upon, embarrassed, ashamed, or rebellious in response. Instead, engage the child in a friendly discussion conducted in a kind tone of voice. It might go as follows:

"Oh, O.K. You think that the sun turns off at night. That's a pretty good idea. It's one way to explain what the sun does. Other people have other ways of explaining what the sun does. Some say that the sun does not turn off, but that it just goes and shines somewhere else—that it makes daylight on the other side of the Earth. Do you think this is a good idea?"

Take your child's ideas seriously. Allow for the existence of more than one explanation or definition. Talk about each explanation as well as about the one that you consider more correct or more reasonable. Ask your child to summarize conversation. You might say: "Okay. Let's summarize." "Whatever were we talking about . . . what was the subject?" "What kind of conversation (scientific, emotional, etc.) did we have about that subject?" "What was the course of the conversation? What happened first, second, etc.?"

Framing conversations and thoughts is yet another way to teach the child to think about thinking. This method also helps build writing skills.

TEACH SPATIAL SKILLS

Spatial ability develops with a child's experience with spaces. It is the ability to relate areas and objects and their shapes and sizes to each other. Although much of spatial learning is learning by doing, there is also a lot to be said for learning by thinking. A child is never too young to hear you ask, "Do you think that will fit there?" This question triggers wondering, contemplation. The child's eyes "see" the situation (the yarn that will or will not fit through the eye of the needle, the puzzle piece that will or will not fit next to another piece, the desk that will or will not fit under the window, etc.). The child's mind then "sees," in another way, visualizes or builds a "mental construction" of the problem.

Babies and toddlers build the ability to visualize, to think about spatial questions by physically handling objects and at-tempting to make them fit. At about 3 years of age, begin asking your child to "see" how something might fit before trying to make that something fit. "Dan, which way do you think we should turn this puzzle piece to make it fit here?" Do not push children this age to visualize a spatial problem. Just suggest visualization to them: "Try to see in your mind how it would fit into the puzzle." Such suggestions open the door to a heightened awareness of this type of mental activity. Six-year-olds are more ready to purposefully attempt spatial problems in their minds. Older children can be pressed to develop more powerful mental abilities by asking them to. By the age of 9 or 10, children should be encouraged to regularly practice visualizing in order to answer even complex spatial questions.

DEVELOP NUMBER SKILLS

The learning of number skills requires the development of both memorizing ability (the building of expertise) and analytical ability (or control knowledge). Basic number facts are eventually memorized through repeated exposure. The control knowledge involved in applying basic facts and analyzing mathematical prob-lems builds with practice.

Life is full of opportunities for mathematical analysis. Take advantage of opportunities to do mathematical analysis with your child. Regardless of the child's age, you can regularly involve your child in counting, measuring, adding, estimating, and other procedures. The older the child is, the more mathematical analysis he or she can do independently of you. As soon as you believe they are up to the tasks, ask children to double-check restaurant bills, calculate the miles per gallon of gas your car is getting, balance your checkbook, calculate the down payment on your house, and so on. If your child is too young to do such things, let your child watch you and, as the child matures, explain what you are doing, again and again. Teach your child as you go along. Eventually, have the child participate, first in small ways, then in big ways. Some children eventually help their parents calculate tax estimates.

USE MUSIC IN LEARNING

Music is the key to the heart, the soul, the mind, and the body. Bring music into your child's life from birth, or, if you are adventurous, from before birth, by putting headphones on the mother's belly, as has been suggested by some prenatal education experts. Even prenatal and newborn infants can feel rhythms. A rhythm is a repeated sound pattern, a repeating beat. Feeling and hearing rhythm from a young age help the child's mind learn to recognize patterns. Because pattern recognition is an essential skill in reading, mathematical reasoning, and abstract thinking, children can benefit by being stimulated with rhythmic music.

Preschool-age children also gain verbal skills by learning songs. Play the same songs again and again for very young children. They begin learning by remembering the tunes and the phonetic sounds that accompany the tunes long before they learn to talk. In memorizing even bits and pieces of songs, the mind of a baby opens storage compartments for future words. More vocabulary can thus be accumulated earlier in life.

Preschool and K–12 children can actually learn to speak and spell more rapidly when music is applied. For example, I wanted my daughter to learn her whole name very young so that she would not learn other people's mispronunciations and shortenings first. Her first name, "Evacheska," is unusual and long and likely to be mispronounced, and her last name, "Browne-Miller," is two names combined by a hyphen and apt to be shortened to "Miller." So when she was about 8 months old, I began singing her whole name over and over again to the French tune "Brother John":

"Evacheska"
"Evacheska"
"Browne-Miller"
"Browne-Miller"
"E" . . . "va" . . . "ches" . . . "ka"
"E" . . . "va" . . . "ches" . . . "ka"
"Browne-Miller"
"Browne-Miller"

Eventually she began humming along and then singing the words. Once she did, I moved to the next lesson: how to spell her name. First, I selected a tune that had been burned into her mind, probably from some TV commercial. (Selecting a tune is important. You must pick a tune you will not forget maybe even for a year or two. You do not want to change the tune on the child as you go along. This is because the child learns the tune and connects the tune with the words.) Then, I put the spelling of her whole name to the music. Each of her names was spelled out in singing form: E-v-a-c-h-e-s-k-a (pause) B-r-o-w-n-e (pause) M-i-l-l-e-r. She learned to spell her whole name quickly, long before she was 3 years old, and never forgot it. (In fact, she recently reminded me of the tune I selected for this lesson years ago.)

EMPHASIZE ORGANIZATIONAL SKILLS

Teach the child to think clearly and in an organized manner. "Easier said than done," I hear replied when I give this advice.

This reply makes sense. After all, how does a parent or a teacher get into a child's mind and organize it?

There are ways. By having your child do organizing exercises in the physical world, you are teaching the child's mind to organize objects. Organizing objects by size, color, purpose, age, value, or other categorical divisions demands that the mind organize ideas and concepts. Take advantage of the real and invented needs for organization. Have your child sort knives, forks, and spoons into separate containers. For young ones who should not handle dangerous utensils, cut up pieces of colored paper into chips. Have them organize chips by color and, as they progress, by particular shades of colors. Children who cannot yet, without your help, sort whatever you give them, should be assisted, never criticized, and always applauded in the organizing work you give them.

RECOGNIZE DIFFERENCES

Learning to identify large and small differences between things is part of learning to think. The organization activities referred to in the above section involve differentiation. Unless one can tell the difference between things being sorted, they will all fall into the same category. Look for opportunities to distinguish between types of dogs, flowers, books, foods, and so on. Look also for opportunities to observe finer differences among flowers on the same bush or among petals on the same flower.

TEACH RELATIVITY

Be sensitive to differences between differences. "That dog and this dog are a bit different from each other, but that dog and that very tiny dog are even more different from each other." When you are on the freeway, talk to your child about how cars are moving at different speeds. Look for cars that are moving at a very different speed from each other. Compare these differences to those between cars going close to the same speed. Talk about the differences between differences as much as possible. This teaches relativity. It creates a slot in the mind for advanced comparison and highly abstract thinking.

HEIGHTEN CONCENTRATION, ALERTNESS, AND ATTENTION SPAN

Find ways to provide your child with concentration training. What types of activities constitute concentration training? Just about anything that requires the mind to stay actively focused on the topic for marked periods of time. (I say *actively* focused here, because activities such as television viewing tend to encourage a more inactive, detached focus and I do not include them in my concentration-training scenario.) People who become highly proficient at something that requires a lot of practice—such as playing the violin, playing chess, or performing ballet—have had to learn to concentrate in order to develop their special skills. Once concentration is developed, the ability to concentrate can be transferred from one subject to another. This ability is especially potent if an individual begins developing it at an early age and continues developing it through adolescence and into adulthood. Here is an opportunity for a parent to influence his or her child's mental abilities: stimulate sustained concentration by training in music or some other activity that requires hand–eye coordination.

Parents do well to encourage (not force, but definitely provide a structure for) their children to learn to be an expert at something. This exercise requires a great deal of mental concentration and commitment over many years. This type of experience gives a child important knowledge about his or her capacity to concentrate. It allows a child to learn (1) repeated, sustained, and cumulative goal-oriented concentration over a long period of time; (2) confidence in his or her ability to focus; and (3) variable concentration skills that can be transferred to other activities undertaken in childhood, adolescence, and adulthood.

Giving a child the experience of long-term concentration aimed at skill development in a single area or a few select areas also allows the child, and later the adult, to feel confident enough to undertake difficult activities. All too often, we do not attempt challenging endeavors because we have never been led to believe that we can accomplish them. We do not believe in our own mental abilities because we have not experienced them.

Another approach to the development of concentration skills is direct training. Again, childhood is the best time to begin learning to concentrate deeply, but it is never too late. You *can* teach even an old dog some exciting new tricks. A few, very few, elementary, junior high, and high schools and colleges are now offering direct training in thinking skills. One of the many thinking skills that *can* be taught, or at least enhanced, in the classroom is concentration. Unfortunately, educators and parents alike tend to overlook the training of the mind to concentrate.

One of the essential elements of any form of concentration training is the understanding of the essence of concentration. Ask yourself what you think the definition of concentration is. Then check your mind out—do it *now*—how closely are you concentrating on what you are reading here? How do you know? What can you do right now to focus in on this reading activity?

You will learn a great deal about your child's mind by studying your own. Survey your knowledge of your own concentration ability as follows:

- Have you ever been aware that you were concentrating intensely on something?
- Exactly how did you come to realize this?

- On what were you concentrating so intensely?
- What types of activities do you concentrate intensely upon?
- Do you allow yourself to be distracted when what you really want is not to have to concentrate?
- Are there particular times of day and places in which you concentrate best?

You can improve the workings of your mind and of your child's mind by learning to concentrate. Your memory will improve. Your attention span will lengthen. Your ability to work with complex ideas will be increased. You will know enough about what concentration is to share it with your child. Concentration skills are immensely valuable in developing intelligence and in building confidence in that intelligence.

STRENGTHEN MEMORY

Memory skills are also invaluable. Memory plays a critical role in learning. Without memory, what is learned is lost. Furthermore, without remembering the simple facts, lessons, and concepts upon which the next level of mental development is built, a child would not grow developmentally. There are many scientific explanations for memory and learning. We can generalize or simplify them here this way: Bits of information are taken into the mind and held in the short-term memory. This information is examined, applied, and repeated until it is assimilated enough to be moved into the permanent or long-term memory.

Memory can be strengthened with practice. Try to build these practice methods into your ongoing interactions with your child (as well as with your own mind):

- Memorize sayings, poems, songs, and the definitions and spellings of long words.
- Remember a series of events in acute detail.

- Remember where things were last seen, especially by retracing your steps.
- Memorize a whole story or a speech.

INCREASE BRAIN SPEED

Brain speed is the speed at which electrical impulses or signals move across the brain from one point to another. Researchers have measured some forms of brain speed with electrodes. Some scientists claim that the more intelligent a person is, the faster the signal moves.

A brain can and should be exercised. Just as you can help your child strengthen his or her memory, you can cultivate his or her brain speed. Runners who sprint in competition practice to increase speed. Thinkers—or any persons using their brains—can practice to increase brain speed. Try activities such as these:

- Find a game or an object that has a light that blinks suddenly. Even a flashlight with a blinker button will do. The child should be required to do something immediately upon seeing the light blinked on. If you are playing a manufactured game, such a requirement may be built in. Otherwise, create opportunities for your child to practice responding as rapidly as possible to a stimulus such as a light that suddenly blinks on. The required response should be an easy one, involving a small motion of the hand. Do this type of practice regularly and begin as young as you can get your child to participate. Children of all ages benefit from such practice, so do not avoid it if you have not started them young.
- Play games that encourage quick thinking. Aim the questions and the demands of the game at the ability of the child. (Do not ask a 1-year-old child to spell "establish-

ment" as rapidly as possible.) Try to select questions your child can actually answer. The goal here is getting answers rapidly, not measuring whether or not the child can get them right. For example, say your child knows basic addition but has learned it recently and is not very fast with the answers. Practice:

> "What is two plus two?"
> ". . . Uh . . . four."
> "Good. One plus one?"
> ". . . Um . . . Uh . . . Um . . . two."
> "Now two plus two again."
> "Four."

Continue this way whenever you find a chance. I am suggesting that you generate a state of mind here: Once you begin looking for opportunities to raise your child's mental abilities, you will find them everywhere. Have fun with this process.

Chapter 10

Learning to Learn

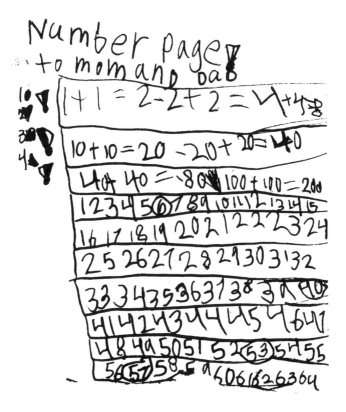

> As a child (between four and seven years old), I saw in the outside world only those objects which were useful to my pleasure. These were above all, rocks, trees, and rarely more than one object at once. I remember that for at least two summers I saw nothing of my surroundings but one large rock which was located about 800 meters from the village, that rock and objects relating directly to it.
> —Alberto Giacometti, artist in
> "Yesterday Moving Sands"

Learning is a creative process. It is also a selective process. The mind creatively selects information to be thought about and then stored. Once information is stored, it has been "learned." Children's minds can be trained to become more attentive to this remarkably creative process of selection and storage, of learning. Children's minds can learn to learn.

In this chapter, I discuss some important aspects of learning and of learning to learn. Read this chapter when you have quiet time in which to think. Parts of this chapter may require some real concentration. If you read these parts again a few times and think carefully about what is being said, it all will come to you, either while you are reading or sometime later. Apply as much of what you read as you can to your understanding of your own thought processes. The more adults know about the process of learning, the more they can make children aware of the process.

Let us begin with the very basic process of *learning to see*, of becoming aware of seeing, of taking in visual information. This will help us understand the way children's minds work when they are learning. It will also help us teach children about how their minds operate. The more children know about the operation of their minds, the better they can cause their own minds to function.

THE AUTOMATIC LEARNING OF ILLUSION

So much of the learning we do is done automatically. While the automatic and subconscious acquiring of information is a valuable and even essential brain function, there is much to be gained by consciously scrutinizing it. If we seek to enhance the learning process, we have to take portions of the learning process off of automatic.

We can gain an understanding of what we learn automatically, unconsciously, by considering the process of seeing. Most of the seeing that we do is automatic. Somehow, quite subconsciously, we manage to learn to see. We also learn to have our minds change the things that we see. Consider the process of "form completion," or what I prefer to describe as automatic form completion. Form completion is an illusion the mind creates. In form completion, the mind provides a whole picture of an otherwise discontinuous or incomplete subject. [1] For example, a picture of a broken circle may be seen as a picture of a whole, unbroken circle. During this form completion event, information about circles is drawn from one's memory, from stored recollections of previous experiences with circles. This information about the true nature of circles is added to the inadequate data regarding the present experience of a broken circle. Clinical tests show that subjects who are shown, in rapid succession, pictures of incomplete circles and other basic forms complete them at high speeds. In fact, these subjects do not know that they are completing the forms. They instead report that they see the incomplete figures as complete or whole figures. The broken forms are mentally completed, automatically fixed, by a process I like to call "not-seeing," the not-seeing of the gaps in the incomplete figures.

We all do a great deal of not-seeing. A very common, but more complicated, version of automatic form completion is taking place every time we see our entire field of vision without gaps, despite the fact that our visual receptors, our retinas, contain blind spots and scars. Our eye movements compensate for our blind spots. By moving while looking at something, our eyes allow all points within the visual field to be "seen" by the retina. However, in any given instant, there are portions of the picture we do not actually see. A whole picture of what is being seen is compiled through this automatic scanning process. We automatically do this type of form completion in order to see. Yet we must admit that our brains are actually fabricating an image, and that we call this fabrication "seeing." What we are really doing is what is defined above as not-seeing—not-seeing the gaps in our incomplete fields of vision. We do this not-seeing in order to see, or at least to convince ourselves that we do indeed see.

Our automatic completion of otherwise partial pictures and fragmented information has true survival value. We learn to do this quite naturally. No one teaches us. It is a built-in function. What this means is that the world we see is an illusion, one that we construct through automatic processes such as form completion. We construct whole images of our otherwise fragmented environments. Although these whole pictures are basically illusions, they are our everyday realities. We must always remember that a child, just as an adult, constructs a personal reality, an illusion that he or she believes, and then lives in it.

Another form of ongoing illusion—not-seeing—is the perception of color. The "seeing" of color is merely a mental translation of incoming data regarding variations in wave lengths of light. This translation is very subjective; it is part of the process of creating a picture of reality. Every perception of color is an illusion. We do not see colors as they really are. For example, two different shades of color can appear to be the same, or two identical colors can look entirely different. [2] An orange may look dull next to a bright red object and much brighter next to a black object.

And so, another one of the parts of reality that we and our children take very much for granted—the specific colors of things—is quite illusory. The differences in colors that we see are just our mental interpretations of what is really out there.

It is important that we share this understanding about the mind's role in creating reality with our children, even the young ones. Our minds are so powerful that they tell us what it is we see in the world around us—even if we do not see it all and we see it inaccurately or inconsistently. Talk about these concepts with children. Show them books with pictures of optical illusions in them. Ask your child to study these optical illusions and to talk with you about what he or she sees in them. What is the illusion? What does the mind think that it is seeing? What is really there to be seen? Get color chips from paint stores. Cut up these color chips and let children see how the same color looks different when the color next to it changes. Over the years, continue to find ways to regularly provide examples of how one's reality is defined by one's mind, how reality is basically a mental construct.

AWARENESS OF CHANGE AND DIFFERENCE

The illusions of form completion and color are part of a larger process of automatically "learning" about one's environment. Most of what we and our children see and know, we see and know because we can tell the difference between it and what is next to it. Our ability to recognize changes and differences in the terrain of our realities is essential to learning. It *is* learning.

Let us return to the process of seeing. Vision problems teach us a lot about the seeing process. Cataract patients consistently report an immediate awareness of a change following an operation to remove their cataracts. Once the cataract is removed, the newly

regained visual field takes on character; it begins to reveal variations in light, color, and detail. Specific colors can be named
within days of the operation. Many patients progress further,
quickly identifying forms and patterns they are beginning to see
again, based on the visual memories they accumulated before they
developed cataracts.

By contrast, a person who has been blind since birth, who
eventually is fortunate enough to undergo a surgical correction of
his or her condition, does not see as readily as do many cataract
patients after their cataract removal surgeries. Unlike the cataract
patient, the individual who has been blind since birth has no sight
to be regained. For this person, seeing is a new experience.
Cataract patients learned to see early in life and thus begin seeing
after surgery more rapidly than patients who have never seen
before. Vision is a *learned* process and it takes time to learn to see.
New learning, new detection of similarities and differences, is
rapid if there is a good foundation or springboard of previous
learning. (Hint: To extend this discussion to general mental
ability, let us say that whatever training we can give a child in
seeing differences will be a springboard for later intellectual
development.)

Seeing is a moldable process. Whether it is seeing or hearing
or smelling or touching or tasting, the process of taking in
information from the environment can be trained. Because seeing
and other forms of sensing can be learned, these processes can also
be refined, that is, learned more precisely, with the right training.
This is a valuable concept for parents and teachers. It takes
learning to a more profound level. Both in school and at home,
children take in information through their eyes and ears (and other
senses). We can teach children how to take this information in
more efficiently.

The way to teach this is to encourage a continuously increasing sensitivity to, and awareness of, detail. Play detail awareness
games, games that involve hunting for differences and details in

meadows, among flowers in the same bush, in faces, in everything you see with your child. Do this frequently. You will find opportunities as you walk, drive, look out the window, and sit in a room together. Close your eyes and do this with sounds some night. Close your eyes and do this while you are eating spicy food.

Understanding the importance of differences and similarities is a critical element in a child's mental development. For example, the more degrees of difference between light and dark shades of gray (or of any color) that can be detected by a child, the more information the child draws from the environment. This sensitivity to differences is basic in sensory perception. [3] Learning to see involves learning to see and to appreciate differences. After all, if no differences at all were perceived by the child, there would be no characteristics of reality detected; no information would be drawn from the environment. The child, blind to all difference, would be unable to function, unable to learn. As a child's awareness of differences increases, that child's perceptual precision increases; the child's learning ability increases as well.*

We can help a child increase his or her perceptual precision (see, hear, and perceive more accurately). We must get right into the process of creating reality, of mapping the environment, with our children. The child (and any living organism) "maps" its environment based on the differences it perceives. Gregory Bateson, who taught ecological philosophy at the University of California at Santa Cruz, explained it this way:

> What is it in the territory that gets onto the map? . . . if the
> territory were uniform, nothing would get onto the map,

---

*It is important to note here that the detection and appreciation of differences do not necessitate the placing of a value judgment on these differences. To avoid the difficulties of certain types of social discrimination, especially racial discrimination, against those who may appear to be different from ourselves, it is necessary to give children careful and regular reminders that differences are often best experienced when they are appreciated.

> except its boundaries. . . . What gets onto the map, in fact, is difference, be it a difference in altitude, a difference in vegetation, a difference in population structure, a difference in surface, or whatever. Differences are things that get onto the map. [4]

Learning to "see" (or hear or feel or taste or smell) is dependent on learning to appropriately map and categorize what is seen (or heard or felt or tasted or smelled) based on differences. This mapping process is basic to learning in childhood. Every young child can recognize (and select) distinguishing characteristics. This permits him or her to set groups of objects, persons, or events apart from other groups. [5]

As a child develops, he or she comes to "know" the world by seeing finer distinctions between things and events—between phenomena. That child is forever improving his or her ability to differentiate by acquiring greater sensitivity to difference. For example, when a young child looks out a window, he or she may not know whether several unfamiliar men are going by, or whether they are all the same man who just keeps reappearing. The child is unable to distinguish between the two possibilities. This is typical of young children. When a small child points to a dog and is told that it is a "doggie," he or she then calls all dogs "doggie." And when the child sees a cat, that child will most probably call it a doggie as well. The child is transferring information from one case to another. [6]

Learning to perceive involves learning to distinguish. Something is not seen (and not mapped, not categorized, not named) until it is differentiated from everything else. The growing child continuously refines this ability to perceive differences, to really "see." This development does not cease in adulthood. We continuously refine our seeing potentials and, with them, our mental potentials. Yet, no matter how many years of seeing we do, unless we can learn to distinguish something, it will remain virtually unseen. The more that we, as adults, work to refine our abilities to see, hear, taste, and smell, the more information we will take in from our environment, and the more we will learn. The more we know what this process is about, the more we can share it with our children.

I have been using the word "seeing" in a relatively literal way, in talking specifically about the process of seeing with the eyes and relating seeing to other sensory processes. But we can also think of seeing as the seeing of ideas. The child learns to "see" differences between concepts in much the same way that the child learns to see objects. The child "sees" the order of ideas, fills in gaps in their forms, and seeks differences between them, just as that child does with visual information coming in through the eyes. Children learn to "see" ideas and to organize them in their minds in terms of their similarities and differences (forming categories and orders of importance of ideas). The more children are aware that they are doing this, the greater their mental power.

LEARNING TO LEARN

Children can thus learn to learn. So let us talk about learning for a moment. Learning is change. Gregory Bateson taught that when a child changes his or her response to a signal or a stimulus, that child has learned. [7] A change in response or reaction or recognition takes place each time something is learned by the mind.

The basis of all learning is the mere receipt of a signal. This has been called "learning-zero." Learning-zero is, actually, "non-learning." Why? Because it does not involve the evaluation of experience. It merely involves the receiving of a signal. Nothing is done with that signal. There is no change in response to the receiving of the stimulus. When a child touches a hot iron and gets burned, and then touches the hot iron again, no learning has occurred after the first burn. This is learning-zero.

The next level of learning, "learning-one," or simple "single-loop" learning, involves the remembering of information and of one's reaction to the information. For example, when the child touches the hot iron, that child's reflex is to remove his or her finger away from the hot metal. When presented with the hot iron again, the child may know better than to touch it. If the child does not touch the iron, he or she has learned from previous experience. In this instance, the first level of learning, learning-one, has occurred.

A higher level of learning is learning-two, or secondary learning: Having learned not to touch a hot iron, the child may be able to transfer the information about this experience to a new setting in which that child encounters a hot stove. If that child can take this knowledge and *generalize* it, that child will know not to touch *any* piece of hot metal or *any* hot utility: This child has now learned to learn. The child has transferred the learning about the hot iron to other hot things.

Children (and adults) can learn to seek opportunities to learn information that they can apply again and again in different circumstances. In this manner, a child can become increasingly sensitive to the value of the things that he or she learns. That child can learn to spot transferability. You can help the child in this process. Having learned to learn once, the child can seek out other simple learning experiences that can lead to other second-level learning experiences. When a child does this, that child has learned not only how to learn but how to learn to learn. That child can now learn to learn at will.

TEACH TRANSFERABILITY AWARENESS

Promote at will your child's development of this learning to learn:

- Begin talking about learning to learn as early as you can in your child's life. If you did not begin in the second or third year of your child's life, then begin now (even the teenage years are not too late).

- Young children may not entirely understand what you are saying, but just keep mentioning the matter of learning and finding examples of the way we learn to learn in daily life. Just hearing you repeatedly identify and define the process causes the child's developing mind to create a space for incoming information about the process. Remember that ideas that are identified and named have a better chance of being remembered. You can help your child identify the specific mental processes of learning to learn.

You open the door to second-level learning when you create opportunities for information transfer. As you create these opportunities, discuss the fact that you are creating them with your child.

- Make up games or puzzles that illustrate information transfer. Ask, for example, if a cat is an animal and a dog is an animal, then what is a horse? Explain that knowing that cats, dogs, and horses have something in common and knowing that cats and dogs are animals make it possible to transfer the knowledge to horses.
- Bring a child into discussions of sequence, such as "Yesterday was Saturday, so today is Sunday." "Tomorrow is Wednesday, so today is Tuesday." Explain that knowing the order of all the days of the week helps one figure out which day comes before or after the other. We all transfer information about the order of days of the week all the time without realizing it. Having learned to transfer this knowledge of sequencing, we apply the ability to sequence in other areas, such as counting, alphabetizing, and so on.
- Use (but do not seek) painful experiences, such as being burned, as the chance to promote transfer. The hot iron burns, so what might the hot stove do? After the child answers this first question requiring the transfer of learning, you can help the child see how information about the

hot iron can be applied or transferred to other hot things. "Anything hot can burn." (For more on this, refer to the discussion of the value of struggle in Chapter 13.)

Infuse your children's thinking with an awareness of the second-level learning, or transfer, process. Climb into the child's thinking process. Be there with the child when the sparks fly from one part of the brain to another. Look and listen for the little or big "aha's" that accompany second-level learning. Children may miss many of their own discoveries. Help children identify these. Point out the occurrence or possible occurrence of transfer whenever you think that it has occurred. Explain what you see and think:

- I think that you have discovered that a lion is in the cat family because that lion looks like a cat.
- You have seen people using forks and spoons to put food into their mouths. Now we are at this Chinese restaurant. You see people using sticks to put food into their mouths. Those are chopsticks. You have figured out that chopsticks are a kind of eating tool too. How did you figure this out? What did you say in your mind?
- You know how to use that computer program. Today I have placed a new program in the computer and you know how to begin exploring it, because you have learned to use the other program before this. What ideas do you bring to this new program from the old one?

Your explanations can become increasingly sophisticated over the years. You will be amazed at how quickly your child will catch up with you and then lead the way. Learning to learn depends on a combination of experience, knowledge, awareness, and positive attitude about the process.

But most of all, someone has to let a child know that learning to learn is possible. Someone has to teach the child to recognize this process. That someone is you.

Chapter 11

Learning How to Think

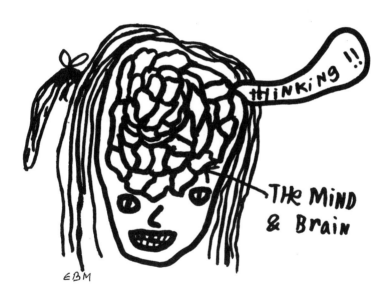

THE MIND
& Brain

thinking !!

EBM

"Oh, help!" said Pooh. "I'd better go back."

"Oh, bother" said Pooh. "I shall have to go on."

"I can't do either!" said Pooh. "Oh, help *and* bother!"

"Hallo, are you stuck?" [Rabbit] asked.

"N-no," said Pooh carelessly. "Just resting and thinking and humming to myself."

"Here, give us a paw."

Pooh Bear stretched out a paw, and Rabbit pulled and pulled and pulled. . . .

"*Ow!*" cried Pooh. "You're hurting!"

"The fact is," said Rabbit, "you're stuck."

"It all comes," said Pooh crossly, "of not having front doors big enough."

"It all comes," said Rabbit sternly, "of eating too much."

—Winnie the Pooh and Rabbit from
A. A. Milne's *Winnie the Pooh*

In this chapter, I focus on the knowledge that young people have about thinking. There is definitely room for instruction in this area. Parents and teachers must teach young people how to think clearly, creatively, and efficiently. I envision an entire niche, a special, permanent, ongoing course, in the K–12 and in the higher education curricula, for instruction in how to learn, how to think, and how to enhance intelligence. This course must be aimed at focusing students' minds on the roles of various mental processes in intelligent thinking. Think about it. We teach specific language and mathematics skills throughout the school years, but not specific thinking processes. The benefits of such an ongoing effort to train young minds in the art and science of thinking could be far-reaching, with the potential of raising the academic performances of our youth, strengthening the power of their minds, and preparing the next generation to move well beyond the progress we expect in the realms of ethics, social organization, science, art, and other human endeavors.

Until such a subject becomes a basic part of all curricula, most individual teachers and parents are on their own: they must assume the responsibility for teaching children to think and to learn. I therefore dedicate this chapter to educating parents and teachers about some very important aspects of the thinking process.

BASIC TYPES OF THINKING

In Chapter 2, I defined two different types of knowledge: "expertise" and "control knowledge." Recall that expertise is also called "material knowledge." Expertise is based on experience in the material, or outer, world. Its purpose is to know a body of specific facts about the material world. Control knowledge is based on what goes on in the mind. Its purpose is to know the process of thinking. [1]

Today, more than ever, knowledge is viewed as an elaborate system of processes instead of just a body of expertise or information. Thinking is viewed as a "complex but understandable process." We are becoming just as curious about the process of getting an answer as we have been about whether or not the answer gotten is correct. A growing emphasis is placed on the process of thinking, on the "control knowledge" described in Chapter 2. We humans are becoming increasingly conscious of what it means to think. We are turning our attention to the levels of thought that were once so automatic that we ignored them. [2] One relatively new field of theory focuses on what it calls "representations of knowledge," or ways in which the mind represents its knowledge to itself. Such theory explains that knowledge is put into a mental code and then stored and operated upon in the mind—in the "intelligent system"—in many ways. [3]

If we can better understand children's (and adult's) thinking processes, then we can teach them how to think and how to learn better. However, we must exercise caution in our efforts to mold children's mental processes. Whether it is in the form of parenting or teaching, we must always remember that, as Andrea di Sessa says, "Education is an interaction with the thinking process and can influence it best by respecting the structure of the process." [4]

What does Professor di Sessa mean by "respecting the structure of the process"? And how can a parent or an educator manage to respect this structure? Begin by thinking of the child's mind as both an information collector and an information processor.

For example, a child learns to identify and name many animals. This expertise is generated by the collection of information from experience after experience of seeing animals or pictures of animals and hearing their names. Eventually, the child learns to group animals by family and species. While some of this grouping ability results from information collection, much of it also involves information processing. The child may think, "Let's see, my cat is a mammal and that cow is a mammal and humans are mammals. They all give birth to live babies and have breast milk to nurse them. My dog does those things too. My dog must be a mammal too." In a very personal way, the mind of the child has worked with, or *processed*, the information he or she has collected. When a parent or educator seeks to respect the structure of the child's personal thought process, this process is not ignored or denied. It is appreciated and built on.

This child could have said, "My cat has ears and is a mammal. That cow has ears and is a mammal. I have ears and they say I am a mammal. My dog has ears, so my dog must be a mammal." This would have been a correct conclusion, but one based on faulty information. Ears are not specific to mammals. Yet respecting the child's knowledge structure means that, instead of shooting it down as wrong, we provide the child with experiences and observations that lead the child to make his or her own corrections. In this case, we might show the child the ears of a bird and tell the child that a bird is not a mammal. And then we might show the child special characteristics of mammals, pointing them out on a number of mammals or pictures of mammals. Live animals are the best teachers in this respect, as they provide the most direct experiences of what we are trying to teach here. However, photos and films will be quite adequate to provide the child with enough information to reformulate his or her own ideas about mammals.

A child accumulates a large quantity of experiences early in life. Your child builds experience-based notions of reality based upon these experiences. Respect the child's experience-based notions of reality. These experiences affect, if not determine entirely, that child's levels of expertise in many areas, as well as his or her own intellectual processes, abilities to learn, and intelligence. Whether or not you or your child's teachers realize it, the process of educating a child involves interacting with a child's preexisting, experience-based notions of reality—of what things are, how they can be organized, and how they can be thought about. Education that ignores these notions of reality does not educate. It does not retrain existing thought processes. It fights with them instead. And it often loses.

The education of children must talk to children's preexisting notions of reality. No matter how childish, immature, and naive these notions may be, teaching is more effective if it works with them. Parents and teachers who proceed as if students' minds are devoid of all previous impressions will have little success. Too many errors are made in this way. [5] All too often, parents and teachers are tempted to assume that the reason for a student's incorrect answers is low intelligence. [6] While this is an understandable assumption, it is frequently incorrect. This assumption is based on parents' and teachers' lack of information about the alternative knowledge structures, the preexisting notions of reality, of their students.

There is a growing body of research, contributed to by Professors Andrea di Sessa and Michael Ranney at the University of California at Berkeley, regarding the development of knowledge and reasoning in physics and related subject areas. [7] Among its findings is that students' "naive" theories of physics affect their understanding of the laws of "expert," or real, physics. [8] This means that the information a science teacher tries to teach often feels wrong to a child. Students arrive in their first physics classes not as "blank slates" in the areas of force and motion but with elaborate and quite naive theories of how things work and move. [9] Although these elaborate theories describe and provide explanations for the behavior of moving objects, they support a host of misconceptions that actually run counter to the laws of physics. Some of these misconceived theories are similar to medieval explanations of force and motion. Many of these explanations have what seem to be childlike qualities in the eyes of expert physicists. Most of the naive explanations of force and motion are shared by many people (including adults) who have not studied physics.

The "naive" explanations I am talking about are made up of specific misconceptions that are highly resistant to change even in the face of contradictory evidence. They have become embedded into the mental system at the perceptual-motor ("gut") level rather than at an abstract level. [10] What our children (and we) know about reality is based on our interpretations of our sensory experiences, and, as I explained when I talked about automatic illusion and not-seeing in Chapter 10, this interpretation is not always correct. Bombs do not drop directly down from moving planes; they curve downward. Water does not gush from a coiled hose in a spiral; it shoots straight out. Yet many people who have had several courses in physics will continue to insist that these things happen. Their reasoning is built on what they believe they have seen to be true. Within their own private knowledge systems, their answers are almost always correct and often intelligently derived.

Old belief systems die hard, when they can be put to rest at all. The process of changing a young person's mind may require a great deal of what Professor Ranney has referred to as a "coherence-enhancing" reorganization among naive beliefs. [11] This reorganization involves providing the young person experiences that are "incoherent," that is, incompatible with his or her naive beliefs. When the child discovers that certain experiences do not fit with the views of reality he or she has fashioned, the child reorganizes from within whatever incoherent (incorrect, illogical, poorly reasoned, uninformed, or disorganized) thinking that child discovers he or she might have.

Proceed carefully. For example, if a young person thinks water gushes out of a coiled hose in a spiral, do not just explain why it does not. Show that it does not. When a young person is taught a new explanation for a physical event or for any other scientific, mathematical, or conceptual event, the teaching must build on what that young person already knows—even if what he or she knows is incorrect. [12] Parents and educators must respect the conflicts between old and new knowledge structures that their children feel. Always keep in mind that what a child is being taught may be clashing with what the child thinks he or she already knows.

Again, what seems to be low intelligence may actually be the expression of intelligent but naive experientially developed assumptions that are incorrect but that have been formed, by your child, into knowledge structures. With help, your child's mind can learn to evaluate and revise the knowledge structures it builds. Naive and alternate knowledge structures can be retrained. [13] In this way, intelligence or intelligent use of information can be learned.

Our understanding of the learnability of intelligence becomes clearer as we gain a better understanding of how knowledge is taken in by the brain. But how much can the mind learn? Can we really teach children to think about thinking? To learn to learn? Yes, we can. However, in so doing, we must realize that a young person comes to any discussion about thinking with his or her own naive and often subconscious, but deeply ingrained, views on the subject.

PROBLEM SOLVING

For parents and teachers to help children learn to think, they must first do some thinking about their own thinking. Ask yourself how you go about solving a problem. What are the steps in your own process? Examine your own thought processes as well as those of others. Among the mental processes students, or any of us, can learn to work with is the all-important problem-solving process. Break this process down into as many distinct steps as possible. Here, below, is my "composite" breakdown, based upon some 400 interviews. I find that the mix of these steps in about this order is increasingly articulated as the age of my subjects increases. However, even 5- and 6-year-olds, in their simpler wording, describe taking most of these problem-solving steps. You may follow a similar series of steps or use a different process:

STEP: *Consider the reason for being presented with this problem*
STEP: *Assess the level of difficulty of this problem*
STEP: *Note your degree of familiarity with this problem*
STEP: *Judge the type of problem*
STEP: *See this problem in your mind*
STEP: *Try it on for size (physical imaging)*
STEP: *Connect this problem to personal experience in the material world*

STEP: *Build on experience*
STEP: *Apply relevant principles*
STEP: *Break the problem into small steps*
STEP: *Build on others' findings*

Do some thinking about each step that you identify. Ask yourself or the child you are working with to select a problem and then:

Consider the reason or context for being presented with this problem. Why are you thinking about this problem right now? Did a teacher assign it to you? Did your parent give it to you to do? Did you find it in a book? Would you handle such a problem differently if you were working on it for a different reason?

Assess the level of difficulty of this problem. How easy or difficult do you think this problem is? How do you know this? If you think it is too hard, are you responding to this problem first with your feelings (emotionally) before you just stop and think carefully about it? Can you tell the difference? This is a problem that you *can* think through to solve. Feelings are very useful, but the best feeling to have right now is one that says "I can think this through clearly. I can think carefully about thinking, and I want to think about problem solving."

Note your degree of familiarity with this problem. Have you been given a problem like this before? When? How often? Do you consider yourself used to, just getting used to, not very used to, or not at all used to problems of this sort? What makes you think so? How do you know this?

Judge the type of problem. Is this a math problem, a science problem, an English problem, or some other kind of problem? How do you know what type of problem this is? What things about this problem tell you what kind of problem it is?

See this problem in your mind. Make a picture of this problem, or something that looks like a part of this problem, in your mind. If you do not have a picture, just make one up. There is no right or wrong here. Any picture in your mind is a good place to start. Or if you can draw or sketch something about this problem on paper, do this first. Then, try to see this sketch in your mind. What would it look like if you saw it on television?

Try it on for size. Imagine that you can walk into this image or picture. Wander around in it. How does it look from the inside? Can you see it from different corners or sides of the inside? What about from various sides of the outside? What we are talking about is physical imaging. We can use our imaginations to act out problems we are trying to solve—to see them. We can use our memories and our imaginations to act out things that we have done before with our bodies—in order to sense the answers to our questions. When we do this, we are engaging in physical imaging.

Look closely at what your own thinking about how something works really depends on. Can you think about other ways that this something might work? Can you see other ways in your mind? Treat it as if it were an object. If it is an object, ask yourself to imagine how it works. What steers it? What happens if you do not turn it on? What happens if it is upside down?

I find that the ease with which I can do physical imaging depends on whether the thing is familiar, perhaps something that I have done before. I reach into my data bank and look for a picture of whatever it is I am thinking about. Say it is a bicycle, and I am wondering how a bicycle really works. I reach into my mind and I find a memory of myself riding the bike. I ride the bike in my mind.

Connect this problem to personal experience in the material world. What sorts of things have you done (games you have played, work you have done with your hands such as building or cooking or drawing or playing with toys) that help you think about problems like this one? Explain how these are connected to this problem in your mind. What activity does this problem remind you of?

Build on experience. Use everything you know to help you solve this problem. Search through your mind for things that might help you but that you would tend to overlook.

Apply relevant principles. Are there specific rules or theories that you have been taught that are useful in thinking about this problem? If so, what are these? How do they apply?

Break the problem into small steps. What do you do (think) first, second, third, and so on in solving this problem? What is the *sequence* of your thoughts? Think in small steps; define specific pieces of the process.

Build on others' findings. If you are working on this problem with another person, or persons, ask each other each of the above questions. Then build on each other's way of solving this problem.

RESPECTING THE PROCESS AND THE STRUGGLE

We can learn to recognize the particular reflexes (including emotions such as confidence and lack of confidence) that we and our children experience when confronted with mental tasks. If we can do so for ourselves, then we can help our children to recognize their own responses to mental challenges.

Try to develop, in yourself and in the child, some degree of awareness regarding the mind's control of its knowledge and the knowledge process. Define in as much detail as possible the steps involved in thinking through a problem. Help the child become especially sensitive to:

- The emotions experienced when confronted with a mentally challenging problem.
- The feelings that arise as one struggles to solve a problem.
- The selection of a particular procedure for solving a problem.
- The organization of the information about the problem.
- The invoking of particular conventions in order to work on a problem (this may be visualizing or imaging a picture, or it may be some other procedure).

The goal here is not getting the answer but arriving at a clearer understanding of the *process* of getting the answer. This includes an appreciation for the valuable sense of struggle that can precede great achievements (whether they are large or small). Go for extremely specific knowledge of the process of solving whatever type of problem you are looking at. Aim for details. Be certain to tell a child, in the appropriate language for that child's age, "You have been able to bring some of the functional parts of answering such a question into your awareness, into words. Now listen to your mind. Your mind talks to you and you have to listen to it very carefully." Help the child incorporate the idea that the control knowledge I defined in Chapter 2 is learnable and that it is a valuable thing to learn. Encourage your child to describe the means that he or she uses to think and to problem solve. Listen for and applaud explanations such as this one offered by a 7-year-old: "Well, you just make a picture in your mind and then you turn it around. If it doesn't seem to fit, then you try it the other way." As your child gets older, the explanations should become increasingly detailed and should be broken into more steps. Encourage this development by explaining that you are looking for this.

The more a young person learns to respond to challenge or struggle with problem-solving methodology, the more control that young person has over the functioning of his or her mind. Somehow, many of us have learned that if an answer does not come to us easily, then we are not going to be able to get it at all.

REFORMULATION

As I noted earlier, the driving force behind all my research in the field of intelligence is my contention that intelligence, or mental competence, is learnable, and that modern K–12 and college curricula ought to regularly and directly address the learnability of intelligence. One of the elements of such intelligence training should be what Professor di Sessa calls "reformulation exercises." [14]

The general purpose of a reformulation exercise is to take a child through a revision, or reformulation, of one of his or her naive (and incorrect) theories. This teaches the child to examine and revise his or her own methods of thinking and problem solving, to learn to learn and to let in new information. The goal is to expand the child's awareness of his or her own control knowledge. In your work with the child, you will have to select a vocabulary appropriate to that child's age. Aim to lead the child to:

- A greater consciousness of the workings of his or her control knowledge.
- The belief that an awareness of one's own control knowledge is the first step in raising one's mental competence and intelligence.
- A sense that control knowledge, and therefore at least one component of intelligence, is learnable.

When you select a problem to be solved or a question to be answered. Allow the child to give you an answer even if it is incomplete or incorrect, in which case you will have something to reformulate. Direct the reformulation conversation in an increasingly introspective direction, getting to exactly how the child is thinking while trying to answer the question. Eventually, ask the original question again.

Say your original question is "What makes a car run?" About two minutes into the discussion of how a car runs, explain that you are interested in your child's answers to this question and also in the mental processes he or she goes through while trying to answer. When you first ask the question, ask the child what is happening in his or her mind. Ask again three to five minutes later.

Then proceed to a new level of conversation in which you ask the child to report what he or she has to say about the question as well as what his or her mind is doing in order to answer the question. Frequently ask something like, "What is your mind doing now?" Continuously aim to reformulate, to increase the child's "grain" of understanding, to sharpen the child's focus on the workings of his or her own thinking process.

OBJECTIVES OF REFORMULATION

Experiment with reformulation over time. You will become an expert as you gain experience:

- *Encourage evolution of the knowledge system*: Rather than simply tell a child that he or she should reconsider or add to his or her definitions of intelligence, let that child observe his or her own mind at work. Encourage the child to draw into conscious observation his or her own mental workings and then to build upon a combination of what he or she already knows and what he or she newly observes. Ask how his or her thinking about this problem has changed during this discussion.
- *Try to understand the intellectual topography*: Attempt to "climb inside" the mind of the child, to see the way that child sees the functioning of his or her own mind.
- *Break mental problems into small pieces*: Aim to break down not just the problem at hand (mathematical, scientific, etc.) but also the larger problem of explaining how a mind works when it encounters such a problem.
- *Keep the learning package small*: Do not take on all aspects of thinking at once. Focus on a single aspect of thinking (a single issue in algebra or in grammar, for example). Present one problem to solve at a time to use as a demonstration.
- *Recognize what is important and what is unimportant, what is*

fundamental and what is random, in this process: Wade through the many comments that do not pertain to control knowledge, always steering the conversation toward control knowledge or at least attempting to do so. Of course, you will not necessarily use the term "control knowledge" with children too young to appreciate it. Call it "thinking about how we think" or do not call it anything.

- *Apply a strategy to engage these fundamentals*: Listen closely for any indication of or reference to the controlling or performing of mental operations on material knowledge. Indications of this include:

    ○ any reference to the organization of ideas or facts in the mind
    ○ any reference to the classification of this problem as being in a particular subject area
    ○ any reference to this problem as being a particular type of problem
    ○ any direct or indirect reference to specific problem-solving methods

- *Note how easily a child will change formulations*: Although many children are prone to disagree about a new explanation, most are surprisingly willing to add new components to their own theories or formulations. The argumentation structures of children are not highly capable of resisting reformulation. This is especially true when children are asked to revise—to reformulate—their ideas about thinking and problem solving. Their views regarding control knowledge or what they know of control knowledge are not at all resistant to reformulation. Perhaps this is because their own problem-solving theories, although seemingly complicated, are not highly developed.

The way a child (or an adult) organizes the process of solving a given problem is part of solving that problem. Quite often, we are not conscious of this level of our problem-solving activities. One reason that control knowledge is so frequently ignored is that it is not talked about. Furthermore, it may be inaccessible in the sense that the child (or the parent or the teacher) does not realize that it is indeed knowledge and that this knowledge can be put to good use. [15] Knowledge processes are so often subconscious. Young people suffer when their parents and teachers do not help them recognize these subconscious processes.

RECOGNIZING CRITICAL THINKING

We must understand, first of ourselves and then of our children, that we create our perceptions of our realities. We create our own thought processes. We select:

- The particular response to any mental challenge or struggle with which we are presented.
- The specific problem-solving methods we apply to any given classroom or life situation.
- The method of encoding anything and everything fed to the brain from the sense organs, which is all noise until it is encoded by the brain.
- The processes of abstract reasoning (thinking) through which we arrive at what seem to be fundamental and undeniable truths about how to spell, how to do algebra, or how to conduct a scientific inquiry or project.

We must also understand and teach our children that:

- Anything received by the brain is recognized only if the brain has a preexisting slot for it.
- The brain determines the structure and organization of thought within the brain.

- Knowledge comes into existence by the organizing efforts of the mind.
- The more elaborate these organizing efforts, the more intelligent the resulting knowledge.

Knowledge without experience is not knowledge we can use in the real world. Even the most complex and abstract of our thoughts are usually built on the simple thoughts we have as a result of our experiences. Deeply buried or subconscious knowledge about thinking without the conscious experience of thinking about thinking is not conscious knowledge about thinking: subconscious knowledge is not conscious knowledge.

It is important that we learn how to think and that we become increasingly conscious of our thinking. We have the opportunity to help adults of the future become highly proficient at this. Learning how to think is much easier for people who were led into the process as children.

Chapter 12

Teaching Creativity and Consciousness Technology

> . . . we could do nothing without the help of my sister. You have
> no idea how wise she is. She has eyes, too! Why, she can see you,
> at this moment, just as distinctly as if you were not invisible; and
> I'll venture to say, she will be the first to discover the Gorgons.
> —Quicksilver speaking to Perseus
> in Nathaniel Hawthorne's "A Gorgon's Head,"
> from Hawthorne's *Wonder Book*

Intelligence finds its way into expression via creativity. We often overlook the role of creativity in the expression of mental activity. Instead, we see only the most obvious signs of creativity, the most innovative inventions, the newest science-fiction films. We notice children's wildest stories, brightest paintings, and loudest projections of their creativity.

Yet creativity is manifested in most every expression of the mind. Just turning an idea into an expression of that idea requires creative energy. Thinking about taking a drink of juice and then lifting the glass to one's lips and sipping the juice requires an ingenious transformation of thought into action. However, this and most simple actions like it are so common and so automatic that we rarely appreciate that transformation. Still, the things we do, the efforts we make, along with those things done and made by all living creatures, constitute the body of creativity. Life is a creative process.

CREATIVITY AND THE SPIRIT

Doctor Maria Montessori, on whose work the "Montessori Method" of education is based (which encourages the child to

learn at his or her own pace—to shape himself or herself), suggested that, "The newborn child should be seen as a 'spiritual
embryo'—a spirit enclosed in flesh in order to come into the
world." [1] Montessori thus described the child as an incarnation
or "enfleshment" of the spirit and explained that, "The incarnation comes at the cost of great inner difficulty, and around this
creative work unfolds a drama that has yet to be written." [2]

What is this "creative work" of incarnating, of coming into a
body in this material plane of reality? It is, perhaps, one of the
most challenging manifestations of one's essence that is ever
undertaken. Yet it looks so easily and naturally done by a baby.
Just eat, sleep, excrete, cry, babble, and gurgle—that is all a baby
appears to do. And even an older child does not seem to most
onlookers to be visibly struggling to manifest his or her spirit.
But what is unfolding in that mind? How many avenues for the
expression of the spirit are being forged within that brain?

We must see the young person as being continuously and
creatively engaged in the expression of the spirit through the
mind and body that he or she is developing. We are most in touch
with our reverence for the mind of a young person when we think
in terms of the spirit it expresses. The creativity involved in this
expression is something we can encourage, nourish, and educate.
However, whatever specific activities we undertake with the goal
of encouraging creativity in our children must be driven by a
prevailing respect for the spirit housed within the body of the
child. This spirit is always creatively working to express—to
manifest—itself.

THE CREATIVITY-ENHANCING ENVIRONMENT

When we seek to encourage creativity beyond what is already naturally present in children, we must proceed from the
assumptions that:

- *All* living things are creative.
- Life is a creative process.
- Even the most simple, common acts are creative.
- All transformation of ideas into efforts or actions is creative.

Again, let me stress that the child in which you wish to encourage creativity is already a creative being. You are merely providing an environment that enhances that natural creativity. Of course, there is a lot adults can do to create creativity-enhancing environments for children:

- First and foremost, adults must model creativity by painting, dancing, storytelling, and anything else that feels and is creative.
- Second, adults must make it clear that the positive use of creativity is appreciated, valued. Notice and approve children's creativity. Acknowledge adults' creativity as well. Be a frequent and willing audience for the expression of creativity through the arts and sciences. Everyone's taste patterns are different. Pick and choose from among a broad range of exhibitions, concerts, plays, and shows; teach children to be good audience members and to appreciate creativity as the adults around them do.
- Third, make a conscious effort to introduce into children's lives activities that are aimed specifically at developing their own innate creativities. Classes in drawing, painting, sculpting, acting, dancing, singing, music, and other creative activities are wonderful experiences for children of all ages.

SEEING RELATIONSHIPS AND CONNECTIONS

Once information has been stored in memory by the brain, it must be retrieved to be used. Retrieval usually involves some form of connection or association between whatever task the individual is performing and the stored (previously memorized) information. For example, if I ask a first- or second-grade child to tell me what eighty-six plus one is, that child may be reminded of other some-number-plus-one types of questions. Knowing that one more than ten is eleven and one more than twelve is thirteen is helpful. Knowing that six plus one equals seven is still more helpful.

The memory "six plus one equals seven" is triggered by the sound of eighty-*six plus one*. The memory of adding one to any number is triggered by the sound of *plus one*. The mind connects the task at hand to previously stored information.

When a more complex task is presented, such as "Think of a living thing that has fins but is not a fish," the mind must recall quite a bit of information:

1. A living thing is an animal or a plant.
2. A fin is a flat, armlike part of some animal's body.
3. Plants do not have fins.
4. Fish have fins.
5. Dolphins and whales also have fins.
6. A dolphin is not a fish.
7. A whale is not a fish.

Now the mind is retrieving several bits of information, each of which it may have learned and stored in memory at different times, under different circumstances, for different reasons. The child might have learned the term "living things" in preschool. He or she might have learned about fins on a family trip to the zoo. Other information may have come in at other times. The child must relate the question being asked to information taken in at other times and then put it all together. As the child gets older and gains more experiences in the world, he or she has more bits of information to connect, and he or she can find an ever-increasing number of relationships among these various bits of information.

Interconnection is most critical in this discussion. The more that a piece of information is interconnected with other information, the greater the chance it will be retrieved, that is, remembered. We can help children become highly conscious of the importance of connecting information by talking to them about how bits of information can be connected to each other. Just talking about connecting thoughts helps a child become more aware of the possibilities of doing so. Make this a recurring conversation over time, over years if you can. This contributes to the building of conscious creativity in the child.

DEVELOPING ASSOCIATION SKILLS

The ability to connect or associate information is applied so frequently and is so very automatic that we rarely think about it. However, this ability, and many of the mental skills it depends upon, can be taught and thus enhanced. When a child is encouraged to consciously connect ideas, that child's conscious creativity is being stimulated. The connection of what may be, for the child, otherwise unconnected ideas, concepts, or images is a creative act. The conscious connection of these ideas, concepts, and images is a consciously creative act. It requires the conscious creation of a link between bits of information.

Teach your child to be highly conscious of the all-important linking process:

- Point out that links can always be made.
- Aim your examples of association or linking at the child's mental level.
- Play association games such as "I'm thinking of something big and red that starts with f." Although you may be thinking of a fire truck, do not hold the child to a particular answer. The goal is to associate and to be creative, not to be right.

- Play sentence and story completion games, and talk about how each player thinks of his or her ideas.
- Play charades, and discuss the thought processes of the players.

INTERDISCIPLINARY ADVENTURES

Children of all ages benefit tremendously when they see how different pieces of information, various subjects, and seemingly separate abilities can be related to each other. Mix ways of learning and knowing together, and relate different academic subjects to each other whenever possible. Use art and music to teach verbal skills in the child's first and then second (or foreign) language. Employ the use of art supplies when teaching children scientific, mechanical, and biological material. When studying history, consider the dress, the music, the food, the art, the family life, and the culture as well as wars and governments of the time being studied. Give children a deep appreciation for the relationship between disciplines by relating the disciplines for the child until he or she takes over. For example, show how geometry is both math and art. If you know music, show how music and math are related by counting out beats per measure and treating each note as a fraction of a pie. Connecting fields of study can spur great intellectual creativity.

FUEL INQUIRY

Did you, as a child, ask what seemed, to adults, to be too many questions? Encourage this asking in children. Inquiry is creative and essential to mental development. When I say this, I hear parents reply that they want to respond to their children's incessant questioning, but that it is just too much and too intrusive and out of control. What I suggest is that busy parents set an official and regular question-answering time. Try very hard to stick to this for a few months and then you will find that this activity becomes a natural, spur-of-the-moment event. Your planned sessions should proceed something like this: The children asking the questions can write down or draw the questions (or if they are too young, their parents and sibling can do this) in order to remember them. If children have saved no questions for the scheduled question-answering session, encourage them to make them up on the spot. Set an example of this inquiry process by making up your own questions. Teach question asking, inquiry, to all children, regardless of their original levels of question asking. Even if a child is not a question-asker, he or she will be inspired by these question-asking sessions or games.

TEACH CHILDREN
THE SPIRIT OF CREATIVITY

Always seek the creative way, choosing innovative, untried, unusual, or different approaches to challenging situations, whether these situations are merely homework problems, logistical issues, or full-blown crises. Demonstrate and encourage the creative spirit, the "I can figure this out" attitude, the belief that the answers are within us all and we need only explore and develop our minds and spirits to discover them.

Solving math problems or brain twisters together with a child is a wonderful way to teach "I can" creativity. Visit your local library, bookstore, game store, or toy store, and select books and games that contain age-appropriate problems. (Many of these will actually be labeled as being designed for a particular grade or age range. Be careful about your choices. After experimenting, you may discover that your child needs something designed for younger or older children. Adjust your selections accordingly.)

Emphasize the fact that there is always more than one way to get
the answer. Courses in creativity frequently place greater emphasis on the number of ways of solving a particular math (or
other) problem rather than on merely getting the right answer to
that problem.

TEACH CONSCIOUSNESS TECHNOLOGY

I am advocating here for the development of a new technology of consciousness. This calls for the teaching of a new form of
intellectual and spiritual awareness—of a new type of mental
discipline—to children. Let me emphasize that this consciousness
technology bears no particular religious orientation. Instead, it is
a science of the mind, one in which the highest of intellectual
potentials is creatively manifested when intellect and spirit
merge.

When this merging takes place, challenges take on a new
meaning. Challenges provide us with opportunities to practice
overcoming them—opportunities to practice being undaunted by
them and transcending them.

This spirit of conscious creativity involves more than new
ways of finding the answers to math and science problems. It is a
way of thinking, of processing information and thoughts about
information. As we and our children train ourselves to become
highly aware of what would usually be our hidden mental processes (such as those discussed in Chapter 10), we become very
sensitive to the technical functionings of our consciousness.

Our children have the wonderful opportunity to learn this
consciousness from us and to then go much further than most of
their parents and teachers with this technical way of thinking
about thinking. Children can—with our guidance—develop
these awarenesses and their attending powers if they begin metacognitive training and awareness while they are young.

TEACH CHILDREN THE GOAL
OF CREATIVE TRANSCENDENCE

Creative transcendence is one of the most special experiences one can have during one's lifetime. Many of the problems we encounter or create for ourselves are encountered or created to provide us with the opportunity to transcend them. As human beings we have a choice. We can either become so overwhelmed by our challenges and problems that we miss out on this amazing opportunity, or we can realize that a problem is a potential-laden situation.

Teach children the goal of practical transcendence. Help them understand that transcendence requires a new outlook on a situation. No matter how unsolvable, bleak, or painful a mental task such as a homework assignment, a test, a term paper, a speech, an accident, or any minor or major crisis may appear, it can be changed by being seen differently. We can and must teach this awareness. Before any changes in a child's perception of a problem can occur, a child must be convinced of the fact that he or she can turn things around! The child must believe in the possibility of transcendence and must understand the process of creative transcendence.

Transcendence is a process that must be studied and practiced continually. No matter what level of understanding a child (or any of us for that matter) reaches, there is always more to be learned. Remember, there is no such thing as a free lunch. Transcendence is hard work. I describe the four phases of transcendence in Chapter 13.

TEACH CHILDREN COMMITMENT

The proper forms of discipline are keys that can unlock great creativity in those who practice them. The discipline of commitment is one of these keys to creativity, and it is a basic element of the consciousness technology proposed in this book.

The most basic condition for overcoming a problem, for meeting a challenge—for transcendence—is the decision to make a commitment to the process of transcendence. Teach children that commitment to the process of transcending a problem does not just "happen." It is not something that one stumbles into. If transcendence were a random, "stroke-of-luck" event, many people would be experiencing it by chance every day. The transcendence process described here requires a commitment to the process. It requires a heartful tenacity and a determination to experience transcendence.

But just how does a young person develop a sense of commitment? It may be easy for a child to get all fired up about some words of encouragement. But excitement and commitment are not the same thing. Excitement is just a temporary high. Commitment is a process of practicing the same thing, every day, for a long, long period of time. Part of consciousness technology is understanding the ins and outs of the mental attitudes that enable the mind to work well. We must look at commitment from this technical viewpoint.

First of all, being committed requires making a conscious decision to be committed. It sounds simple, but many people, young and old, find that this initial decision is a difficult one to make and to hang on to. Making and keeping decisions takes practice. Decision making is something a child and any one of us learns by actually making and then keeping the decisions made.

Help your child experience the process of commitment by guiding him or her in this exercise: select a week in which to study commitment. Have your child make a week-long commitment to something—to brushing teeth, studying math, learning to spell a new word every day, exercising, or something else of his or her own choosing (not yours). On the morning of the first day, ask your child to make a conscious decision to be committed. Ask your child to wake up that morning and make the decision to do whatever it might be and then to really feel committed to that decision for a day. Then, the next day, ask your child to wake up and make a conscious decision not to be committed and to feel that lack of commitment for the entire day. On the third day of the week, repeat the first day: decide to be committed, and again really feel that decision for all of that day. And on the fourth day, repeat the second day: decide not to be committed, and again feel that experience all day. Continue this on–off, committed–uncommitted exercise for two more days. This will total six days. The child will learn about commitment by experiencing the contrast between commitment and the absence of it. Discuss this contrast as you conduct this exercise. Repeat this exercise each time a new commitment to do something is made.

What this exercise does is train a young person to tell the difference between having made a decision to be committed and having made a decision not to be committed. As he or she learns to tell the difference, you will see that the child's sense of commitment gains clarity and strength.

When a young person is clearly able to make a decision to commit himself or herself to transcendence, he or she will have overcome a major stumbling block. Many people (young and old) who consciously practice the transcendence process are interested in the profound personal, spiritual, emotional, and intellectual change that transcendence entails but are still somewhat afraid of that change. Because of this fear, they hesitate to truly commit to the process of transcendence. Making a commitment to the process is the first step on the road to transcendence.

To achieve transcendence, one must pay attention. All too often, commitments are made and strongly felt, but a clear and continuing attention to the commitment is not maintained. To learn transcendence, the student must pay tuition—in the form of paying attention. Below are some pointers that will help your child learn to pay attention. Word these in an age-appropriate way so that you can teach your child:

- *When your mind wanders, refocus it*: Your mind will wander away from your commitment. There will be times when you will not notice that your mind has wandered until an hour, a half a day, a day, a week, a month, or perhaps even a year has gone by. Don't let this discourage you. As soon as you notice that your mind has wandered, refocus it. Focus your mind as if it were a lens whenever you realize that it has slipped out of focus.
- *Seek intentional awareness*: Awareness of your surroundings does not happen by accident. You must choose to be aware. Awareness must be intentional, and this requires that you pay attention to what you are seeing and perceiving. Without intentional awareness, there can be no transcendence. So *pay attention*.
- *When a difficulty arises, generate fortitude*: As you are working on a problem and your commitment to overcoming that problem, both unforeseen and predictable difficulties may arise. Unless you learn to use these difficulties, they will interfere with your struggle for transcendence. You can take any obstacle or problem and use it to generate strength. You can use that obstacle as an opportunity to grow. You can turn it around. Use it as an opportunity to practice feeling fortitude and as an opportunity to increase the intensity of that feeling with each new obstacle. Remember: use your problems to strengthen your fortitude.
- *Keep the faith*: Faith is the ultimate condition for creative transcendence. Without faith in the process of transcendence and in oneself, there will be doubt. Doubt can be hidden or obvious, subconscious or conscious. Whatever form it takes, it undermines the flow of energy into the transcendence process. The feeling of faith is subtle and may be difficult to experience in the beginning; with practice and patience, faith grows stronger.

Children who learn, early on, the practical aspects of conscious transcendence—the technology of conscious transcendence, such as the technical aspects of commitment and the attention, fortitude, and faith that support it—become well equipped to meet intellectual challenges with strong spirits.

ENCOURAGE FREEDOM OF THOUGHT

Discipline and practice are essential to maximizing a child's conscious creativity and in building his or her readiness to apply creativity to challenging mental problems. However, these efforts should not take the form of brainwashing.

Seek to raise independent thinkers. Let your children know that it is acceptable to think differently from the crowd—to choose different clothes, books, movies, and political points of view. It is also acceptable to move at one's own pace through the learning process of life.

Freedom is one of the greatest and yet most elusive qualities of life that we can pass on to our children. And freedom of thought is the key to freedom. Children can learn, must learn, that there is more than one way to solve or transcend a problem, to see the world, to feel, and to think. Make this a topic of conversation through childhood (including adolescence). Parents sometimes shy away from this endeavor because they fear it encourages rebellion. It may do so, to some extent, but the level of rebellion a particular child expresses will not be increased significantly by this ongoing conversation. The questioning of authority is an essential skill in a functional democracy. So is respect for authority. Let your child hear and see you doubt particular ideas, laws, and politicians. Let your child understand that while you exercise your right to think independently, you respect the process and structure of society.

Chapter 13

More Consciousness Technology

The Roles of Self-Esteem and Spiritual Struggle in Intelligence Enhancement

"O Tiger-lily!" said Alice, addressing herself to one that was waving gracefully about in the wind, "I *wish* you could talk!"

"We *can* talk," said the Tiger-lily, "When there's anybody worth talking to."

—Alice talking to the flowers in
Lewis Carroll's *Through the Looking Glass*

Whatever else is said about the enhancement of mental ability, self-esteem must not be overlooked. A young person's sense of self affects that child's expression of his or her mental ability. Generally, the better a child feels about himself or herself, the better he or she will do with mental challenges. The lower a child's self-esteem, the more that child will stifle, suppress, and withhold high performance. Basically, a child rises to a challenge when he or she has enough self-esteem to believe that he or she can meet that challenge.

Why does low self-esteem interfere with performance? The answer is most obvious when it comes to public performances, actions that involve other people—people who are watching. Whether it is being onstage, speaking in front of a group or a class, or raising a hand for the teacher to call on, if a child feels shy, unworthy, ugly, or incompetent, that child will be reluctant to perform. If this child performs at all, the result will be less than the best he or she can do. The child will perform in a manner that reflects—and even substantiates—his or her diminished sense of self-worth.

The answer is much less obvious when we look at what we might call less public, more private performances. These include activities that are not done before the watching eyes of a group or a teacher or parent. More solitary activities such as writing alone, doing puzzles, reading to oneself, and drawing are also affected by low self-esteem. Although the child may feel less direct pressure in the absence of an audience, the child may nevertheless feel a silent pressure to perform and an unspoken sense that his or her performance will never be adequate.

Silent pressure comes from all directions. The first source of silent pressure is closely related to public performance pressure. If anyone will be evaluating the work (such as a teacher does when grading), or hearing about the quality of the work (such as parents do when they see report cards), or competing with the quality of or grade assigned the work (such as some classmates and siblings do), then the work or its results are eventually going to become public performances. Knowing this, a child may be inhibited in much the same way that he or she might be on stage. The audience is definitely out there; it is just a delayed one.

There are other sources of silent pressure. Even when the results of whatever the child is doing will not be witnessed or evaluated by teachers, parents, siblings, or classmates, the child may evaluate his or her own work much as a critical audience would. The child may have experienced evaluation in the form of grades or comments and been uncomfortable with it. He or she may have taken in, internalized, the demand to do a good job from the social and family environment and then, seemingly voluntarily, turned around and placed this expectation on himself or herself.

THE CHILD AS SELF-CRITIC

Many children become quite critical of themselves regardless of the support they glean from their parents and teachers. Children are very perceptive and learn to make comparisons early in life. I discussed this matter with a 9-year-old girl who compared herself unfavorably in every way with her 18-year-old sister:

"She's smarter than me, has more friends than me, is prettier than me, and taller than me. I'll never catch up." I asked this sad girl if things might change as she moved into her high school years. "No," she replied assertively, "I started out behind and that's where I will stay." No matter how hard parents try to avoid the development of such self-deprecating views, these views can develop. And this is not just competition between siblings. I remember when my daughter, at 3½ years of age, began comparing her own painting and drawing to mine. She insistently repeated that Mommy was better at painting than she, that she was not at all good at it. This was somewhat disconcerting, as I, in my love for drawing and painting, had shared my hobby with her regularly from an early age and her artwork was highly advanced for her age. I had never made any comparisons between her work and mine, and I was always complimentary and encouraging. Eventually, she passed through this stage but has remained capable of intensely scrutinizing her own work. While she has developed a good eye, and perhaps the making of a good art critic, she has also demonstrated to me that children will be critical of themselves regardless of what their parents do.

TEACH "I CAN"

Early in life, children see, hear, and feel their parents' attitudes toward themselves. Children mimic much of what they see in their parents. So, parents' levels of self-esteem have a great deal of influence upon those of their children. If a child sees in his or her parents confidence and competence, the child will seek to mimic this. If the child sees instead fear, shyness, timidity, and a low sense of self-worth in the parent, the child cannot help but mimic this.

Children who see their parents not necessarily as perfect or as high achievers but as people who believe in themselves, who believe that "they can," will learn this attitude. Parents who want to and try to teach their children to believe in themselves, to think positively and to say "I can" instead of "I can't," must set an example.

If you have not been setting the "I can" example, remember that it is never too late to begin. You can teach your child a great deal by telling and *showing* your child that you have decided to change your attitude. You might say something to the effect of the statements below, rewording them to fit your own child's vocabulary and maturity level:

- For a long time I thought I couldn't run five miles, but now I know that, if I want to, I can. I am writing a practice plan that starts me at one-half mile and has me at five miles by the end of the year.
- I thought I was not a good speaker, but now I know that I can be a good speaker. I just need to practice before meetings.
- I am going back to school and I know I can do a good job and pass all my classes.

Setting an example is one of the best ways to teach the "I can" attitude. While you are doing this, try another teaching method. This is the gentle restating of a child's negative statements into positive ones. Let's take a simple example to demonstrate the process. When you hear "Mommy, I can't spell 'cat,'" you can suggest that your child say, "I *can* spell 'cat' with some practice" or "with some help." Try suggesting this rewording gently: "Maybe you can say that this way . . ." Do not do this in an argumentative, contradictory fashion. Simply restate, quietly, what has been said. If the child needs a demonstration of what you mean, you can make the sounds of each letter in "cat" and help the child get the correct letter after each sound. When the child has successfully spelled "cat," compliment the child.

Use the same approach whenever you catch an "I can't" attitude:

- Restate the "I can't" in the positive form of "I can."
- After you assess the practicality of the effort you are about to make, demonstrate that whatever it was that could not be done can indeed be done. Do this by coaching your child in doing whatever the "I can" statement says can be done— again and again—or, if the task really cannot be done, by taking portions of it that can be done and helping the child do these. Be patient and stick to your coaching efforts.
- If no part of the task can be done by your child, do not force the child to struggle to meet unrealistic expectations. Instead, find something similar but more simple that *can* be done and focus on this, explaining that this is what one does to learn to do more complex tasks.

Eventually, your coaching on the spelling of "cat," and later, on the spelling of other words, will not be needed. Eventually, you will hear your child say "I can spell 'cat.'" You may hear this even before the child spells cat correctly or entirely independently of you. Let this attitude go unchallenged, unless, of course, the child is repeatedly using the wrong spelling and repeatedly assuming that it is correct.

Whether it is spelling, writing, adding, doing algebra, riding a bicycle, using a computer, or performing some other activity, your child needs to believe that he or she can do it. As your child grows and learns certain tasks, no matter how small, applaud these achievements. You may think adding one plus two is easy, and so may older children, but remember that this is a big step for a child who has never added before. Your ongoing approval, which is internalized by the child, is esteem building.

FAILURE AS A LEARNING EXPERIENCE

Failure is a part of the learning process. Some of us stumble, or fail, more than others along the way. Each of us has our own life path to follow and walks our own special and often jagged learning curve. Children will learn to appreciate this view of life's challenges if you teach them to do so.

Failure has a different meaning for each child. Describe failure, whether it is flunking a test or a grade or getting one word wrong, as a necessary part of life. Even successful students fail. A straight-A student who gets her first B in twelfth grade may be deeply impacted by this experience. Self-esteem among high achievers is fragile. High achievers tend to become attached to this laudatory definition of themselves and then to expect from themselves a certain level of performance. And they tend to be the first to criticize themselves when they do not live up to their own expectations.

STRUGGLE AS A LEARNING EXPERIENCE

Somehow, many of our young people think that life is supposed to be easy. As a result, they avoid tackling anything that appears too hard, whether it be a more advanced level of mathematics, a demanding science project, a longer term paper, a higher quality of academic performance, or anything intellectually or morally challenging.

The illusion that life is supposed to be, or should be guaranteed to be, easy is damaging to many young people. When life is not easy, when the going gets rough, they feel cheated, unworthy, injured. But who ever said life is supposed to be entirely pain free? Is the complete absence of struggle the ultimate purpose of our lives on Earth? Would we learn very much during our lifetimes if everything came easily to us?

I am certainly not justifying human suffering. I agree that much can be done to alleviate and to prevent the suffering that humans cause their fellow humans. However, I am saying that we must view life's difficulties—especially the ones that seem hard to avoid—as special opportunities to learn and grow. This philosophy will foster a higher level of intellectual, psychological, and moral behavior in our young.

Whether it is coping with failure or some other form of struggle, the problematic or challenging experience can be a positive one. The adults in a young person's life must cast difficult experiences in a positive light. The best means of doing this is by working from the standpoint of the consciousness technology that was defined in Chapter 12. A technical understanding of the role of struggle in personal and intellectual development will make it possible for a young person (and for anyone) to develop much further, to realize much more of his or her potential. This is part of the new technology of consciousness that I am advocating in this book.

Alerting a young person to the inherent value of struggle is a practical task. This is not to say that we should ever try to deny the pain that comes with some struggles. Feelings are valuable. They keep us from becoming machines; they preserve our humanness. Yet there is a practical understanding of struggle—and of its pain—that can help children learn to cope with mental and other life challenges. A basic message must be taught from the time a child is very young and must be continuously expressed to that child throughout his or her life: When we treat the process of struggle as a technical issue, as an issue that is best explained in terms of the workings of the consciousness, we can find great value in it. But in what way can struggle be technically understood?

A TECHNICAL UNDERSTANDING OF STRUGGLE AND TRANSCENDENCE

If parents and teachers can make the following ideas about struggle and transcendence part of their teachings, part of daily and weekly life, children will grow up thinking in these terms. These ideas are general enough that they can be applied to a broad range of life's difficulties, from school problems to social problems to confidence problems to handicaps to other minor and major crises.

The ultimate form of learning is transcendence—transcendence of a situation or challenge or difficulty or problem or crisis—transcendence of any form of struggle.

Transcendence is a process composed of four phases:

- *Struggle*: the tough, often emotional and painful, roller-coaster type of experience in which there seems to be continuous difficulty in coping with or solving a problem no matter how hard one tries or thinks that one tries or tells others that one tries.
- *Paradox*: the no-hope, give-up, no-way-out, no-escape, no-answer, darned-if-you-do and darned-if-you-don't, trapped sense that one can get when confronted with a problem or a struggle with a problem. The no-solution paradox often hits after some time has been invested in the struggle.
- *Insight*: a small but all-important transcendence of the problem in the form of the arrival at a sense of competence and confidence, the finding of an answer, the completing of a project, or the experiencing of a burst of energy with which to respond to, address, or cope with a particular problem.
- *Spiritual–intellectual elevation*: the transcendence of more than one piece of a problem or of more than a small problem, or the transfer of the insight to other problems or other parts of the larger problem at hand, a transcendence that is usually accompanied by a change in the way one sees problems of a particular sort or sees oneself or sees the world.

Children may benefit from a translation of these ideas into age-appropriate wording, such as the following:

- Struggle = having a real hard time
- Paradox = the no-answer feeling
- Insight = a good idea or right answer
- Elevation = a big solution and change

ELABORATING THE PHASES OF TRANSCENDENCE

Each phase of transcendence has its own special characteristics and it is important to carefully explain the nature of each phase to young people. I have explained these here in terms an older child can understand:

Phase 1: Struggle: Every day we struggle in a small or large way—perhaps with other people, with family relationships, with school assignments, with ourselves, with morality, with our health, with our tempers, with our moods, with living up to what we or others would like us to live up to. We often struggle without recognizing or seeing beyond our struggles. We become so deeply caught up in them that it becomes impossible to step back and say, "Oh, I am struggling. This must be the phase of transcendence called 'struggle.'" But it is just this observation that will set us on the path to transcendence. When we are struggling, we must take the time to tell ourselves that we *are* struggling and that struggling is valuable because it is the first phase of transcendence. During a true struggle phase there must be low points in order for there to be high points—both extremes are integral to struggle.

Phase 2: Paradox: Paradox is a fantastic experience. It can be painful. It can be frightening. It can be deadly. Paradox is the experience of being in a situation from which there seems to be no

escape, no resolution. The person in paradox feels trapped. Sometimes parents offer children paradoxes in the form of a double
bind. A double bind might go something like this:

"Which coat do you like?" a parent may ask a child. "The red
coat or the blue one?" If when the child says, "The red coat," the
parent says, "That's not a good choice, you should like the blue
one." And when the child says, "The blue one," the parent says,
"Well the red one is much better." When this happens the child is
experiencing a double bind. In this case there is nothing the child
can do that would be the right thing to elicit a positive response
from the parent. The child is bound by an unpleasant consequence
no matter which choice he or she makes. There is no escape. He or
she is bound to a situation that holds, or so it would seem, no real
choices. This is just an example. In life, both children and adults
create double-bind situations for themselves with or without the
help of other people.

Paradoxes like this are extremely stressful and often painful.
But faith in the transcendence process shows us that paradox
serves a purpose. Without the tension, the feeling of being
trapped in an unwinnable situation, there is no impetus for
moving on. The tension created by our paradoxes, when used
well, can generate enough energy for us to break out of the traps
that paradoxes seem to be. Without the pain of paradox, we
cannot experience the release—the jump or shift in perception
that is produced by breaking out of the double bind. The paradox
signifies the "stand off" or "holding pattern" in which one who
needs to grow and experience transcendence gets caught or traps
oneself. The only way out of this holding pattern is to grow past
it, to break out of it and move on, to see beyond its limits. When
one sees beyond the limits of a paradox, beyond the state of mind
that keeps one caught in it, it is no longer a trap.

Phase 3: Insight: Insight is a profound experience. But insight
often comes in small packages. Sometimes we experience insight
without even realizing it. You may be driving along and suddenly

realize something about a problem that has been bothering you. Or you may be working on a project—perhaps a science project or a writing project—and suddenly figure out an unexpected solution. All at once a new idea comes into your mind. You suddenly discover a new way of looking at a problem. This is an insight. It represents a peek into a higher level of experience. But insight is just a peek. It does not automatically bring growth. In order to grow, insight must be recognized and sustained. When insight is sustained, then spiritual–intellectual elevation becomes a reality.

Phase 4: Spiritual–intellectual elevation: Spiritual elevation signifies a jump in perception. This jump is actually an insight that is *sustained*. The self, the soul, or the spirit rises to a new level of being and holds on to this level. This "holding on" to a new level of being or of perception is the experience of sustained insight. Without this experience, the insight is usually brief and the person experiencing the insight returns to or close to his or her original way of seeing the world. Spiritual–intellectual elevation differs from insight in that there is no falling back into one's previous way of seeing things.

From the new level of being that is achieved by spiritual–intellectual elevation, each of the phases of transcendence may have to be repeated to achieve further spiritual elevation. One can always discover new struggles, new paradoxes, and new insights to generate further growth.

Be certain that you and your children understand that each phase may be a few seconds long or may last for years. Some people struggle all their lives. Others live in a perpetual state of paradox. Some rotate between struggle and paradox. Perhaps these people reach spiritual elevation at death. Some people have insights and do not recognize or sustain them and thus continuously return to the same paradox that produced these insights. It is important to explain to children that:

- The phases of transcendence link together in various patterns. The patterns you live can repeat themselves again and again in various ways:

> struggle-struggle-insight-struggle,
> struggle-struggle-insight-struggle,
> struggle-struggle-insight-struggle, or

> struggle-struggle-paradox-struggle-insight,
> struggle-struggle-paradox-struggle-insight,
> struggle-struggle-paradox-struggle-insight, or

> struggle, insight, struggle, insight, elevation,
> struggle, insight, struggle, insight, elevation,
> struggle, insight, struggle, insight, elevation.

- You can change these patterns by learning to see, by becoming conscious of what your patterns are. Your entire experience of living is transformed the moment you identify the phase of this process that you are currently experiencing, whether it be struggle or paradox or insight or spiritual–intellectual elevation.
- With awareness and practice, you can learn to move through each of life's struggles into paradox and then into insight and even on into elevation (a greater form of transcendence):

> struggle →
> paradox →
> insight →
> spiritual–intellectual elevation

or, in a younger child's terminology:

> *Having a real hard time*
> can lead to
> *the no-answer feeling,*

which can lead to
a good idea or right answer,
which can lead to
a big solution and change.

There are many ways to encourage transcendence. One of the best ways is to spot struggles and encourage a new way of seeing them. For example, it may be that some troubled individuals actually choose their struggles as an opportunity to learn to transcend. And where there is truly no choice regarding whether or not one experiences a particular difficulty in life, one still has the choice as to how one struggles and how much one struggles. We decide how we see our realities. Young people may find this concept difficult to understand at first. Why would one *choose* a struggle by fighting with a friend or having a very hard time with math or getting sick or injured? Do not force this viewpoint on a child. Instead, repeatedly remind the child that there are many different ways to view the same problem. Talk to the child about this. Why not see a problem as a challenge? As an opportunity to learn? Tell your child:

- Remember that the transcendence we are describing is a process that gains power as it progresses. Progressive transcendence can overcome any challenge in some manner and then move beyond it. There is no endpoint to this process.
- One must work to maintain the insights and spiritual elevations gained in the process of transcendence.
- With every full cycle of transcendence comes an entirely new way of seeing the self and the world. Be ready and open to total change and a new view of life again and again.

Remember, as you lead your child into the technology of conscious transcendence, that each of us follows his or her own life pattern. However, no one pattern is written in stone. If we were taught as children to recognize these phases of transcendence, then, as adults, it would be much easier for us to see where we were in the process and to take conscious control of it. But no matter how old we are, we can always learn to harness the energy produced in each phase to move on to the next phase. We can learn to see our struggles as fertile ground for astounding growth. We can learn to appreciate paradox, recognize insight, and strive for spiritual elevation. If you keep trying to see this pattern in your own life you will eventually understand that you are already on the path of transcendence. The gift of life will then make itself very clear to you, and become something you can teach.

Teaching the consciousness technology of transcendence to children will not only enable them to raise their self-esteem and to realize their mental potentials, but it will bring about a major change in the world. As the human species becomes more aware of its ability to consciously choose to transcend its struggles and patterns in the physical world, it will ascend to the realm of the spirit. Access to this height of awareness requires a merging of intellectual and spiritual technologies. It is essential that every one of us commit to such an advancement of consciousness technology. Both personal and planetary pressures are calling us into action.

Chapter 14

Building People
for Tomorrow

Children's Life
1. That thay have fun
   What's fun?
1.1. Play ground
1.2. Singing
1.3. Having toys
1.4. Tobe with their mom

By:

Eratheska

2. They like Schod
Why?

2.1. they Like their
teachers
2.2. frinds
2.3. Learning

3 problems they have
what are they?
3.1. my bsent-minded
mother Sometimes
3.2. or fathers
3.3. getting in fights
with friends
3.4. problems at
school

"That's a long time ago," said Wendy. "How time flies."
"Does it fly," asked Jane, "The way you flew when you were a child?"

Wendy smiled and said she sometimes wondered if she ever really did fly. But Jane was certain Wendy had.

"Why can't you fly now?" she asked.

"Because I'm a grown-up now," said Wendy. "When people grow up, they forget. No one can fly when they grow up. You have to be young, innocent and a little selfish to fly."

—Wendy to her daughter, Jane,
in J. M. Barrie's *Peter Pan*

This book has offered parents and educators the view that a child's potential is highly moldable and not set in stone. I have explained some of the basic arguments about this view that philosophers, legislators, scientists, and other citizens make and are influenced by. It is, of course, tempting to be lofty and theoretical about it all. But parents and teachers must wade through all the theory and all the debate, choose what they think is valuable, and then go on with the very direct, front-line work of parenting and teaching.

Parents must try to see themselves as their children's defense against institutions. No one has a greater interest in the success of an individual child than does his or her parent. Until a child is old enough to respect and to protect his or her own interests in the development of his or her own mental ability, the parent must be the protector. Too many children get lost in the educational system, dropped or overlooked along the way. This is what the parent must prevent. The parent must be the protector and then be the advocate. Being the advocate means standing up for a child's right to learn, to realize his or her potential. Sometimes the parent must go to school and do the advocating. Sometimes the parent must do the advocating at home. There are so many social and psychological pressures and distractors on a young person (including peer and media pressures to rebel against authority, to focus on fads, and to drink and use drugs), that someone must advocate, day in and day out, year after year, for the development of that young person's mental potential.

WHAT I WANT TO BE

As I have said, parents are not alone in the molding of their children's minds. Siblings, friends, teachers, television, and many other participants in children's lives have at least as much influence. Yet parents are central to the development of their children's mental abilities. And they are central to the development of their children's awareness of their own mental abilities.

Parents are the front line—the people best situated to help their children realize their own power. How much of what a child thinks he or she can achieve can actually be achieved? Is a child really able to realize his or her dreams? Does the child even dare to dream? Whether actively building answers or passively assisting in these areas, parents are contributing a great deal to children's answers to these questions.

Given that even noninvolvement in the development of a child's sense of power is involvement, a parent may as well elect to purposively contribute in a positive manner. This means more than contributing to the esteem building discussed in Chapter 13. This is a conscious effort to share in the dream-building process, to let a child know that he or she can become a teacher or an astronaut or a president or an opera singer.

Mom and Dad must believe in the child to teach the child to believe in himself or herself. A parent's greatest and most distinct effect on the child's sense of power comes in the first nine or ten years of that child's life, and especially in the years from four to eight. These are the years when dreams about the future can still be aimed high and can still be underscored with confidence that they can come true. "What I want to be when I grow up" is as much reality as it is fantasy in these years. A famous singer, a fireman, a doctor, a mother, the president of the country—these are all still of equal possibility, if and only if a child has been exposed to these possibilities.

FEED THE DREAM

So how can adults feed children's dreams for their own futures? What kind of guidance works?

- Get involved in this process at an early age. And then stay involved.
- Have an "I can" attitude, about your own life as well as about your child's life.
- Expose your child to a range of options. The life of your child belongs to your child, not to you. You can lead your child to the water of opportunity, but you cannot make him or her drink.
- Let your child know that you believe that anything is possible. Avoid saying, "You will never achieve that. You aren't good enough."
- Teach planning and organizational skills from the beginning. These skills blaze a clear trail through the jungle of stimuli, distractions, obstacles, and competing possibilities of life.

Feeding children's dreams requires demonstrating the process of making dreams come true. Do not in any way support the notion that just wishing to be a symphony conductor without studying music is possible. Explain that dreams can come true when we think clearly about how to get from the moment of now

to the realization of the dream. There are many steps, practical
activities requiring real work along the way. Let your child see
this view demonstrated in his or her parents' and teachers' lives.
Show your child how you and those around you go about realizing dreams. Look at the hurdles and rewards of pursuing a dream
together.

DEVELOPING YOUNG CHILDREN'S POTENTIAL

It is difficult to feed dreams of the future to underdeveloped
minds. Parents and educators must begin empowering children's
minds at a very young age. Early childhood is a very critical
period. From birth to age 3, a child undergoes intensive brain
development: there are rapidly forming connections among brain
cells and related growth of brain capacities. The first years of life
are thus the years in which the young mind is most receptive to
stimuli and to learning. Research suggests that approximately 80
percent of all the connections among brain cells are formed by the
age of 3. Within the first six months of life, the child's brain
capacity may reach as much as 50 percent of its adult potential. By
age 3, this capacity reaches 80 percent of that potential.

At about the age of 4, the primary developmental emphasis
shifts away from the formation of sensory and neural pathways,
most of which have been occurring in the hind-brain. Now comes
the very important frontal-lobe phase of the child's brain development. The connections formed during this phase are dependent
on the quality of the cerebral "hardware" forged during the first
three years of life. [1] The mental abilities being developed during
this and later phases of mental development depend on the quality
of the earlier brain development.

The great cognitive potential of early childhood is supported
by all kinds of research and by many parents' and teachers'
experiences. Young children can learn to operate and program

computers. [2] Young children can learn an astounding array of complicated things: to play violin and piano through methods such as "talent education" or the "Suzuki method," to solve intricate mathematical problems, to speak foreign languages, and even before they can talk clearly, even to read foreign and ancient languages. [3]

As I mentioned in my warnings about "superchild" consciousness in Chapter 7, we must not get carried away here. An increasing number of parents feel far too much pressure to provide a concentrated preschool education instead of child care for their children to prepare them for the competition of later life. Special preschool programs, toys, computer programs, and parenting seminars are being established by responsive entrepreneurs who know about the pressures parents feel. [4] Still, what young children need most is *good care*. Some parents overlook affectionate attention in order to give their children educational advantages even before kindergarten. They place their children in preschool programs that focus almost entirely on academics such as geometry, Latin, violin, and computer operation, denying children ample opportunities to play and to love and be loved. It is amazing what pressure and competition will drive parents to do.

Yet some of the pressures parents feel are very real. The gap between children who have been exposed to intensive, professionally designed, "hi-tech" education and those who have not is definitely increasing. Everywhere, I see the advantages that children from superb academic preschools have over children who have not had such preschool experiences. Do not let anyone tell you that it makes no difference what kind of mental stimulation a child gets in early childhood. It makes a great difference. If the mental stimulation occurs in a group or school setting, the young child is gaining in two ways—via the stimulation itself and via the preparation for the school experience. However, stimulation that translates into pressure to achieve can be quite damaging in a child's early years. We walk a fine line here. Children's minds have so much unrealized potential. How do we unleash their mental abilities without breaking their spirits and their hearts?

SOCIAL RESPONSIBILITY

Another problem with favoring good early childhood education is that not every child has access to it. Most working parents struggle just to find openings in any form of child care, whether or not it is educational. A good preschool that offers education of some sort often has a long waiting list. In some urban areas, parents "apply" to preschool two years in advance of the time they plan to have their children attend. And, all too often, parents who desire educational stimulation for their children simply cannot afford it.

My view is that we, as a nation, lose out by not beginning public elementary school education in the early childhood years. We lose too many minds, waste too many intelligences. We drain, or fail to develop, the intelligence of our society and of our species.

The expression of human intelligence is environmentally determined. To support this view, I have, in this book, discussed many attitudes and methods that promote the expression of mental ability. I have proposed that we teach the next generation a new technology of consciousness. We can and must create a societal environment that maximizes the expression of *all* our children's mental abilities. A technical approach to thinking will facilitate this effort.

Because a child's environment is such a powerful determinant of that child's expression of intelligence, the expression of intelligence and the social power it brings can be made available to all citizens. Why should the expression of mental ability remain restricted to elite portions of the population? The survival of the species depends on the enhancement of the intelligence of a critical mass of its members. Ensuring all citizens, including very young children, the absolute best education possible should be our number one policy priority. We must not go on wasting, by failing to realize, the great potential of our children's minds.

CURRICULUM AS A STRATEGY

A K–12 curriculum designed to teach specific thinking and problem-solving processes must become a standard and explicit part of all school programs. The overall purpose of this curriculum should be fourfold:

1. To fully develop the intellectual and creative potentials of all students.
2. To generate in all students strong awareness of and appreciation for the creative, problem-solving, reasoning, and specific metacognitive abilities of their own minds.
3. To regularly use the metacognitive understanding and awareness gained in academic (school) work and to find applications in daily life.
4. To motivate all students to realize their mental potentials.

Among the many specific classroom activities that must be included in a curriculum of metacognitive consciousness technology at all levels of K–12 schooling are the following:

- Lessons in the process of overcoming problems and meeting challenges, which include a breakdown of the process of transcending them.
- Lessons in the recognition and appreciation of intellectual (and emotional) struggle as a mind- and personality-strengthening event.
- Lessons in reading, understanding, and following instructions.

- Lessons in task analysis, in which students are taught to analyze instructions, assignments, and other tasks in order to break them down into specific sets of steps in specific orders.
- Lessons in temporal relations, in which the sequence of particular sets of events in time is carefully observed and recorded in pictures, words, and numerical data.
- Lessons in memorization, in which students are taught memorization techniques and are given many, many opportunities to practice.
- Lessons in concentration, in which students are given training in concentration and tested again and again in settings where a great deal is done to distract them from whatever it is they must concentrate on.
- Lessons in detecting large and small differences between objects, colors, sounds, notes, bits of information, grammar, concepts, and theories.
- Lessons in the identification of information that is irrelevant in the answering of particular questions, in the completing of particular assignments, in the building of particular models, and so on.
- Lessons in categorization, in which students group like objects or ideas together and then organize them by level of generality, with the biggest categories being the most general and containing the most subcategories.
- Lessons in formal debate, in which students learn to find and argue the strengths and weaknesses of information and theories of a scientific, philosophical, ethical, or political nature.
- Lessons in visualization, in which students use their imagination to generate images of a real objects or geometrical forms in their minds.
- Lessons in the manipulation of actual and conceptual objects and images, in which students learn to "see" or "sense" the

way things will fit together or relate to each other in space, with the aim of improving visualization skills.

- Lessons in the detection of patterns, in which students learn to tell the difference between what we call "noise" or random signals and what we call real "information," the latter of which is generally pattern based.
- Lessons in specific forms of metacognition, in which students study themselves thinking and solving problems, "watching" closely the way their minds work.
- Lessons in getting mental work done, such as homework and class work, in which students learn to keep their workspaces and binders neat, organize their time, plan activities in the present and in the future, and prioritize these activities.
- Lessons in the fundamental arguments of philosophy, for example, rationalism versus empiricism, and practice in discussing these concepts.

It was the introspective seventeenth-century philosopher René Descartes who wrote, "I think, therefore, I am." Whether or not one absolutely agrees with this absolutism, it is increasingly apparent that "The *way* I think, and the *power* with which I think, determines much of what I have and can become."

A MIND IS A TERRIBLE THING TO WASTE

Yes, we have heard it said that a mind is a terrible thing to waste. Yet, how often do we avoid the implications of this adage in our own lives? A child's mind will develop as far as it thinks it can develop. This means that for a child to realize his or her own mental potential, the child must:

- Be led to believe that the potential exists.
- Be encouraged to develop and realize this potential.

- Be provided the stimulation to develop this potential.
- Be provided the awareness that mental challenges and life's struggles help to develop this potential.
- Be provided the consciousness technology, spiritual structure, tools, training, and education to develop this potential.
- Be taught to see the rewards, the value, of mental development and of realizing one's mental potential.

If you see to it that the above elements are present, you can teach your child to realize his or her mental potential. Stay on the case at home and at school. In fact, it is your responsibility to teach your child to be intelligent. Not only is it your responsibility to your child but to your society and to your world.

Adults are the caretakers of the spirit of the future. We give birth to the next generation. What an awesome responsibility and what a fantastic opportunity! Remember the old adage, "The way to a man's heart is through his stomach"? Well, our children are very hungry! Hungry for meaning, hungry for personal contact, hungry for opportunities to express what goes on in their minds. The ultimate way into the child's mind is through the child's spirit. When a connection is made directly with the child's spirit, the mind can surpass even the greatest of expectations. We must guide our children to fuller realization of themselves. We must teach them to believe in their unlimited abilities. They must come to know that their abilities are worth developing. To meet the challenges of the future, our world needs all the intelligence it can generate. *Tempus fugit.*

Notes

Chapter 1

1. R. Sternberg, "A Framework for Understanding Conceptions of Intelligence," in R. Sternberg and D. Detterman, eds., *What Is Intelligence* (Norwood, NJ: Ablex Publishing, 1986), pp. 4–5.
2. H. Gardner, *Frames of Mind: The Theory of Multiple Intelligences* (New York: Basic Books, 1983), p. 368.
3. Ibid.; Sternberg, pp. 4–5; B. Davis, *Storm over Biology* (Buffalo, NY: Prometheus Books, 1986); L. Kamin, *The Science and Politics of I.Q.* (Potomac, MD: Lawrence Erlbaum, 1974).
4. For an overview of this research, see R. J. Sternberg, ed., *Human Abilities: An Information-Processing Approach* (New York: Freeman, 1985), pp. 14–17.
5. L. Humphreys, "Intelligence: Three Kinds of Instability and Their Consequences for Policy," in R. Linn, ed., *Intelligence: Measurement, Theory and Public Policy* (Urbana and Chicago: University of Illinois Press, 1989).
6. Gardner, p. 368.

Chapter 2

1. A. Di Sessa, "On Learnable Representations of Knowledge: A Meaning for the Computational Metaphor," in *Cognitive Process Instruction* (Philadelphia: The Franklin Institute Press, 1979), p. 240.
2. Ibid.
3. M. Chi, R. Glaser, and E. Rees, "Expertise in Problem Solving," in R. Sternberg, ed., *Advances in the Psychology of Human Intelligence*, Vol. I (Hillsdale, NJ: Lawrence Erlbaum, 1982), p. 8.

4. Ibid.
5. Di Sessa, p. 239.
6. Di Sessa, p. 239.
7. Di Sessa, p. 241.
8. Di Sessa, p. 241.
9. Di Sessa, p. 239.
10. This person based his views regarding mindfulness on J. Goldstein, *The Experience of Insight: A Natural Unfolding* (Santa Cruz: Unity Press, 1976), pp. 36–37.

Chapter 3

1. B. Davis, *Storm over Biology* (Buffalo, NY: Prometheus Books, 1986).
2. T. J. Bouchard, Jr., and M. McGue, "Familial Studies of Intelligence: A Review, *Science* 212 (1981), pp. 1055–1059. Note that a comprehensive international analysis of the literature on the correspondence between measured intelligence and familial relationship (which included 111 studies) reported average correlations of .42 between parent and child living together, .50 between child and "midparent" (the average of the two parents) I.Q., .47 between nontwin siblings reared together, .72 for midparent–midoffspring (average of two parents as correlated with the average of the children of those parents), and .31 for half-siblings reared together. See also H. Storfer, *Intelligence and Giftedness: The Contributions of Heredity and Early Environment* (San Francisco: Jossey-Bass, 1990), pp. 68–69, summarizing findings of the Texas Adoption Study, the Colorado Adoption Study, the Transracial Adoption Study, the 'First' Minnesota Study, and the Stanford Adoption Study. Note also that the average correlations between adopted children and adopted parents are .16 for one adopted parent and .19 for midadopted parent's I.Q. These studies also indicate that I.Q.'s of adopted mothers correlate more highly with those of adopted children than do I.Q.'s of adopted fathers, and there are greater correlations on verbal measures than nonverbal measures.
3. Storfer, pp. 68–69; Bouchard and McGue, pp. 1055–1059; S. Scarr and L. Carter-Salzman, "Genetics and Intelligence," in R. Sternberg, ed., *Handbook of Human Intelligence* (Cambridge, England: Cambridge University Press, 1982); L. Erlenmeyer-Kimling and L. F. Jarvick, "Genetics and Intelligence: A Review," *Science* 142 (1963), pp. 1477–1479; J. C.

Loehlin and R. C. Nicols, *Heredity, Environment and Personality* (Austin: University of Texas Press, 1976); R. C. Nicols, "The National Merit Twin Study," in S. Vandenberg, ed., *Methods and Goals in Human Behavior Genetics* (Orlando, FL: Academic Press, 1965); T. Husen, "Abilities of Twins," *Scandinavian Journal of Psychology* 1 (1960), pp. 125–135.
4. R. Sternberg, ed. (1982), op cit; see all articles in this book.
5. R. C. Lewontin, E. Rose, and L. J. Kamin, *Not in Our Genes* (New York: Pantheon Books, 1984), pp. 116, 125, 127.
6. B. Davis, *Storm over Biology* (Buffalo, NY: Prometheus Books, 1986).
7. R. Rosenthal and L. Jacobson, *Pygmalion in the Classroom* (New York: Holt, Rinehart & Winston, 1986).
8. L. Kamin, *The Science and Politics of I.Q.* (Potomac, MD: Lawrence Erlbaum, 1974); Rose Lewontin and L. Kamin, pp. 116, 125, 127; F. Boas, *The Primitive Mind of Man* (New York: The Free Press, 1939), p. 199; also, N. Wiener, "The Great Ravelled Knot," *Scientific American* 179, no. 5 (1948), p. 17; S. L. Lightfoot, *Worlds Apart: Relationship between Families and Schools* (New York: Basic Books, 1978), pp. 191–192.
9. H. Gardner, *The Mind's New Science: A History of the Cognitive Revolution* (New York: Basic Books, 1985), p. 383.
10. Ibid.
11. Ibid.
12. Ibid., p. 86.
13. A. Browne-Miller. *For Whom the Bell Tolls* (Ph.D. diss., University Press, University of California, Berkeley, 1992), p. 207.
14. Gardner, pp. 86, 383.

Chapter 5

1. A. Browne-Miller, *The Day Care Dilemma* (New York: Plenum, 1990).
2. Ibid.

Chapter 7

1. S. Pringle and B. Ramsey, *Promoting the Health of Children: A Guide for Caretakers and Health Professionals* (St. Louis: C. V. Mosby, 1982).
2. Ibid., p. 1.

3. B. Vanderberg, "Play Dominant Issues and New Perspectives," *Human Development* 24 (1981), p. 357.
4. J. Mander, *Four Arguments for the Elimination of Television* (New York: Quill Publishing, 1978).

Chapter 8

1. E. Hale, "Good Nutrition for Your Growing Child," *FDA Consumer* 21, no. 3 (April 1987), p. 23.
2. A. Browne-Miller, *Transcending Addiction and Other Afflictions* (Norwood, NJ: Ablex Publishing, 1993).
3. S. White and B. N. White, *Childhood: Pathways of Discovery* (San Francisco: Harper & Row, 1980), pp. 70–71; see also R. J. Lemire, *Normal and Abnormal Development of the Human Nervous System* (New York: Harper & Row, 1975).
4. D. J. Greenberg, I. C. Uzgiris, and J. McV. Hunt, "Attentional Preference and Experience: 3. Visual Familiarity and Looking Time," *Journal of Genetic Psychology* 117 (1978), pp. 123–135.
5. M. D. Ainsworth, *Maternal Deprivation* (New York: Child Welfare League of America, 1969).
6. C. A. Doxiadis, *Ekistics: An Introduction to the Science of Human Settlement* (New York: Oxford University Press, 1968), p. 327.

Chapter 10

1. W. Dember, *The Psychology of Perception* (San Francisco: Holt, Rinehart & Winston, 1973), p. 195.
2. E. Gomringer, *Joseph Albers* (New York: George Willenborn, 1962), p. 104.
3. G. Bateson, *Steps to an Ecology of Mind* (New York: Ballantine Books, 1972).
4. Ibid., p. 451.
5. K. Yamomoto, *The Child in His Image* (Boston: Houghton Mifflin, 1972), p. 36.
6. Ibid.
7. Bateson, pp. 279–308.

Chapter 11

1. A. Di Sessa, "On Learnable Representations of Knowledge: A Meaning for the Computational Metaphor," in *Cognitive Process Instruction* (Philadelphia: The Franklin Institute Press, 1979), p. 239.
2. Ibid., pp. 239–240.
3. Ibid., p. 240.
4. Ibid.
5. M. McCloskey, "Naive Theories of Motion," in D. Gentner and A. Stevens, eds., *Mental Models* (Hillsdale, NJ: Lawrence Erlbaum, 1983), pp. 318–322.
6. J. Clement, "A Conceptual Model Discussed by Galileo and Used Intuitively by Physics Students," in D. Gentner and A. Stevens, eds., *Mental Models* (Hillsdale, NJ: Lawrence Erlbaum, 1983), p. 338.
7. McCloskey, pp. 318–319.
8. Clement, pp. 335–336.
9. Clement, p. 337; McCloskey, p. 321.
10. Clement, p. 337.
11. M. Ranney, "Contradictions and Reorganizations among Naive Conceptions of Ballistics" (Paper presented at a meeting of the Psychonomic Society, Chicago, November 1988), p. 2.
12. M. Ranney and P. Thagard, "Explanatory Coherence and Belief Revision in Naive Physics," in *Proceedings of the Tenth Annual Conference of the Cognitive Science Society* (Hillsdale, NJ: Lawrence Erlbaum, 1988), pp. 426–432.
13. Di Sessa, p. 241; McCloskey, p. 320.
14. Di Sessa, pp. 239–266; A. Di Sessa, "Phenomenology and the Evolution of Intuition," in D. Gentner and A. Stevens, eds., *Mental Models* (Hillsdale, NJ: Lawrence Erlbaum, 1979), pp. 15–31.
15. Di Sessa, "On Learnable Representations," pp. 239–266.

Chapter 12

1. M. Montessori, *The Child in the Family* (New York: Avon Books, 1956), p. 29.
2. Ibid., p. 35.

Chapter 14

1. M. Ibuka, *Kindergarten Is Too Late* (New York: Simon & Schuster, 1977), p. 24.
2. S. Papert, *Mindstorms: Children, Computers and Powerful Ideas* (New York: Basic Books, 1980).
3. For example, see M. Montessori, *The Discovery of the Child* (New York: Ballantine Books, 1967); G. Doman, *How to Teach Your Baby to Read: The Gentle Revolution* (New York: Random House, 1964).
4. "Bringing Up Superbaby," *Newsweek*, March 28, 1983, pp. 62–68.

Index